An Education in Georgia

An Education

*Charlayne Hunter,
Hamilton Holmes, and
the Integration of the
University of Georgia*

in Georgia

BY CALVIN TRILLIN

Foreword by Charlayne Hunter-Gault

BROWN THRASHER BOOKS

The University of Georgia Press   *Athens and London*

Published in 1991 as a Brown Thrasher Book
by the University of Georgia Press, Athens, Georgia 30602
© 1963, 1964, 1991 by Calvin Trillin
Foreword to the Brown Thrasher Edition © 1991
by Charlayne Hunter-Gault

Printed and bound by Thomson-Shore, Inc.
The paper in this book meets the guidelines for
permanence and durability of the Committee on
Production Guidelines for Book Longevity of the
Council on Library Resources.

Printed in the United States of America

95 94 93   P   5 4 3 2

Library of Congress Cataloging in Publication Data
Trillin, Calvin.
    An education in Georgia : Charlayne Hunter,
    Hamilton Holmes, and the integration of the University of
    Georgia / Calvin Trillin.
        p.   cm.
    Reprint with new introd. Originally published:
    New York : Viking, 1964.
        ISBN 0-8203-1388-2
        1. University of Georgia—Students—History.
    2. College integration—Georgia—Athens—History.
    3. Hunter-Gault, Charlayne.   4. Holmes, Hamilton,
    1941–   . I. Title.
    LD1986.T75   1991
    378.758'18—dc20   91-23282
                                                      CIP

British Library Cataloging in Publication Data available

An Education in Georgia was first published in slightly
different form in 1963 by the *New Yorker* and subsequently
in 1964 by Viking Press, New York.

For my parents

Foreword

By Charlayne Hunter-Gault

I⊤'s difficult for me to remember exactly when I first met Calvin Trillin, not because it was thirty years ago when our paths first crossed but because my first two days at the University of Georgia as one of its first two black students, admitted by federal court order, were the closest thing to a surrealistic dream I have ever experienced—starting with the first moment I set foot on the campus, walking through its black wrought-iron entrance gates past a boisterous, if not hostile, crowd of white humanity.

It was my impression that most of the people in the crowd were Georgia students, but there were also a lot of reporters, and I'd be willing to bet that Calvin Trillin was moving quietly and unobtrusively among them. That was his way—a way that allowed him to hear and see things that others often didn't, because no one suspected that he was listening and watching. It was a natural demeanor—owed no doubt to his native Missouri—that allowed him to exploit the inclination of the whites around him who assumed that all decent God-fearing people (as opposed to "them damn Yankee outsiders in the press") were on the same side and that you could feel free to say whatever was on your mind at the time, including things like "make way for the nigger" as I walked through the crush.

It was the same everywhere I went in those first couple of days. Students yelling epithets, reporters shouting questions. And me trying my best to look straight ahead to where I was going.

But as caught up as I was in getting from one place to the next without stumbling or otherwise losing my dignity, I was also trying to see out of the corner of my eye exactly what the reporters were doing and how, because, after all, that was why I had pressed this case and was now on this campus in the middle of this throng. I wanted to be a reporter; Georgia had the only school of journalism in the state, and here I was at the center of one of the biggest stories in the country, if not the world. I wanted to see how the real pros did it.

I watched the reporters in action around me on the campus and listened carefully to the questions they put to me. I didn't get to watch the televised reports. In those days, I didn't know of any black women, or men for that matter, working for any white newspapers or in television. All the serious journalists I knew worked in print. I knew there had to be some serious journalists in television, but one incident colored my impression of all of them, at least for the time being. It happened one day when a network correspondent arrived at a location on campus where I had been briefly surrounded by a crowd of jeering students. The incident was all over by the time he got there, and I had long since gone. But not to be outdone by the television crews on the scene at the time, this correspondent asked the students who were there to reenact the scene. They obliged. In those days, stories like that made my blood boil and made me even more committed to print. Obviously, I've changed my mind about television, but not about that kind of television journalism.

For a while, I didn't have any favorites among the reporters. Lillian Smith, author of the classic southern novel *Strange Fruit,* had come to Athens and interviewed me for a national magazine. I enjoyed meeting her, because I had read her powerful book about lynching and I liked many of her observations about injustice and racial inequality. But, I was uncomfortable with the way she interviewed me. She would make a statement like, "Well, I think it's the women of the South who are the ones that will change things, don't you?" And I was worried—perhaps overly so—that if I agreed, the quote would then go into my mouth. It wasn't something I could be sure of; but since most of the conversation consisted of her views, I was more than a little worried about what she was going to quote from me. Maybe it was just her style. She was, after all, a novelist. This was one of the many interviews that helped convince me that, when I became a journalist, I would keep my views to myself.

Then, too, Autherine Lucy, the first black student admitted to the University of Alabama five years earlier, had been expelled for publicly criticizing that university. And "Hamp" (Hamilton Holmes) and I had been warned by our attorneys to be careful. No one wanted some bogus issue to derail our legitimate claim that we had been denied admission on the basis of race.

I mostly read the Atlanta *Journal* and Atlanta *Constitution,* but I also read *Time* magazine. I'm sure I hadn't met Calvin Trillin when he filed his first pieces. They had been written in the aftermath of the weeklong December '60 trial in Athens where Federal Judge Bootle heard our case that had been pending since 1959, our senior year in high school. The other was a January 13 piece called "Break in Georgia," where *Time* reported that Judge Bootle had "ordered the University to admit immediately a 'qualified' Negro boy and girl," pointing out that "their entry will crack the total segregation of all public education, from kindergarten through graduate school, in Georgia—and in Alabama, Mississippi, and South Carolina, as well."

The five-paragraph story in the education section seemed to have the facts right, but in that report I mostly liked the picture of myself seated next to Hamp. And there was nothing in those reports that struck me enough to want to meet the reporter.

But one day, shortly before eight o'clock on a cold January morning, trench coat flapping in the wind, hair falling down over his eyes (he had more hair in those days), notebook in hand, and a gentle smile as he caught my eye, Calvin Trillin stood waiting as I went to my psychology class in Meigs Hall, campus escorts in tow.

He introduced himself as "Bud" Trillin—I don't think I've ever heard him or anyone else who really knew him call him Calvin—and it seemed the perfect name for this completely unpretentious and self-effacing "man from *Time*." In fact, I think it was his lack of airs, of self-importance, that led me to trust him almost immediately. He may have had views of his own, but he always seemed more interested in mine. And in those days, at nineteen, I had plenty!

That night a crowd assembled outside my dormitory at Center Myers Hall and began chanting things like "Two-four-six-eight! We-don't-want-to-integrate!" and "Nigger go home." While I wasn't prepared for that, it didn't surprise me either. It had happened at other schools going through the same transition—Little Rock, University of Alabama—and besides, I was still in that surreal, dreamlike state.

It was my first night on campus and, just as I had approached my first day, I was trying to treat it as routinely as possible. Still, I was startled when someone knocked on my door and announced that I had a phone call.

I didn't know what to think, and in that moment a thousand thoughts rushed through my head. . . . Who knew how to call me at Center Myers? I didn't even know the number myself. Maybe my mother. Or Don Hollowell, one of my attorneys and the one I was closest to. Or Carl Holman, the Clark College English professor-turned-activist who helped us prepare our applications so that the University could not find anything to suggest we were not qualified—like an undotted *i* or an uncrossed *t*. As Trillin was to report, the Georgia officials had asked Hamp if he had ever visited a house of prostitution or a "beatnik parlor" or "tea house."

So I stepped outside my room to the phone in the hall with some trepidation and picked up the receiver.

"Hi. It's Bud. How'd you like to have a pastrami sandwich?"

I was too relieved for words. All I could do was laugh.

"You having a good time in there, kiddo?" he asked, and of course I unburdened my soul. In the end, I declined the pastrami sandwich, but I went back to my room feeling that I had a friend out there somewhere.

I saw Bud a lot over the next few weeks, and I read what he reported—the riot that erupted the night after his call; our suspension "in the interests of [our] own safety and the safety of the more than 7,000 students at the University," as *Time* was to report it; the court order readmitting us; the aftermath—but I especially liked how Bud had woven that psychology class I attended after first meeting him with the events that later unfolded.

He wrote: "In her first class at the University of Georgia last week, pretty Negro coed Charlayne Hunter, 18, heard a psychology lecture on human behavior. The subject was timely, for that morning she and Hamilton Holmes, 19, breached a sorry human behavior barrier: the 175 year old tradition of segregation at the campus in Athens."

Every now and again during those difficult days, Bud would

catch me on the fly and ask me why I wanted to go to journalism school. A good journalist has to be able to write, first and foremost, he would argue. Why didn't I just major in English as he had done at Yale and, like him, learn the rest of the job?

But I was learning . . . and much of what I was learning about being a good reporter was from Bud's example. In fact, Bud Trillin may have been my first *real* role model, Brenda Starr being the *actual* first. From Bud Trillin I learned lessons that have been invaluable to me as I have gone about the business of being a reporter and becoming a journalist, a process that is ongoing.

I learned from Bud that reporters have to go where the story takes them, whether into the middle of an angry white mob or to the pew of a black church in some out-of-the-way southern town during an over-long civil rights rally—listening and observing, ever alert to the ridiculous or the sublime. (Bud, by the way, was best at being alert to the ridiculous, especially when it involved language. For example, he loved the mixed metaphor of some anonymous segregationist who described the desegregation order as " . . . the long arm of judicial tyranny grinding us under the heel of its boot.")

I also learned from Bud that a reporter doesn't have to be distant to be fair; and that it helps to have a sense of humor, as well as a sense of history; and that there's nothing wrong with using your own moral compass, right along with your note pad and pencil. (I never saw Bud use a tape recorder. I think he thought they were for sissies.)

After things settled down on campus, Bud returned to Atlanta, where he was based, and eventually to New York City. We stayed in touch. Once when I had a project to do for one of my journalism classes, I called him—collect, of course—and asked him to have *Time* send me a bunch of promotional materials. I was designing an ad campaign to sell *Time* on Mars. Bud thought it was a dumb idea and told me so, but a few days

later I was inundated with stuff from *Time*'s promotion department. I got an A-plus on my project. Dazzled 'em with props.

When Bud told me he wanted to return and write a book
about our two-and-a-half years at Georgia, I wasn't in a very
good mood. Every now and then, the isolation of the place just
got to me, even without anybody bothering me directly. Bud
was one of the few people I felt I could let my guard down
with, so I told him to come on, as much for my own therapy as
for his project.

Some months later, I flew to New York for an interview at
the *New Yorker* offices. The editor, William Shawn, and the
editor in charge of hiring, Leo Hofeller, had been following my
days at Georgia and knew of my desire to become a reporter.
Many young men and women just out of college—in the *New
Yorker*'s case, it was usually Bryn Mawr or Vassar, Harvard or
Yale, or some other "good" Eastern school—were hired as editorial assistants or other low-on-the-totem-pole jobs. It was
then up to them to demonstrate their other capabilities. When
I went for the interview, I was told that I too would have to
start at the bottom but that I could rise as high as my talents
could take me. The rest of the time we spent talking about
what my life had been like the past two-and-a-half years.

Close to lunchtime, Mr. Hofeller's phone rang and the call
was for me. It was Bud. Before leaving Georgia, I had called
him and made arrangements to see him when I finished my
interview. He was calling now because he was worried that
something might have happened to me. When I hung up, I
explained to Mr. Hofeller who Bud was, told him about his
plan to take leave from *Time* to do the book about Hamp and
me, and mentioned why Bud was calling. I also sang his
praises as a good reporter.

"As fate would have it," I remember Bud saying on the
phone a few weeks after I had returned to Georgia, "the *New
Yorker* is going to run the book as pieces before it's published

and this is going to be my first piece as a staff writer for the magazine."

I couldn't believe it. Fate indeed!

Not long after that, sitting behind my desk at the *New Yorker,* stuffing rejection slips into envelopes and daydreaming about becoming a "Talk of the Town" reporter, one of the fact-checkers showed up with a galley proof that contained the first of the three installments of "An Education in Georgia."

I read it with both trepidation and relish, and when I had finished I knew that I had done the right thing. Bud Trillin had told a story that captured a turning point in the history of the South. And he had told it through the people who had lived it, black and white, good, bad, and in between. There were many wonderful things about "An Education in Georgia," including facts I had not known that detailed the lengths to which the state of Georgia had gone to prevent Hamp and me from getting the education we were entitled to have. But I think the real triumph of the book was that I recognized myself and everyone I knew. And that, for me, was the ultimate test of a good journalist, even if he was only an English major.

Author's Note

THIS book first appeared in January of 1964, at a time when people who now prefer to be called blacks or African-Americans preferred to be called Negroes and when college students of any race were commonly referred to as boys or girls. The text has not been altered for this edition, which means that the language of that era remains intact. It also means that the lives of Charlayne Hunter and Hamilton Holmes are frozen in 1964. Charlayne Hunter-Gault now lives in New York, where she is national correspondent for the MacNeil/Lehrer News Hour on PBS. Hamilton Holmes, an orthopedic surgeon, is the medical director of Grady Memorial Hospital in Atlanta and associate dean of the Emory University School of Medicine.

An Education in Georgia

1

By May 17, 1954, when the United States Supreme Court declared racial segregation in public education unconstitutional, most Southern states had already desegregated their state universities, some voluntarily and some under a prophetic series of Supreme Court rulings on the practical inequality of "separate but equal" education. After the 1954 decision, some of the states had to pretend that the Negroes attending their universities with whites did not exist; otherwise, a good deal of the oratory of the late fifties would have been impossible. In 1957, for instance, when Governor Orval Faubus of Arkansas decided that the enrollment of a dozen Negro students in Central High School in Little Rock would, as surely as election follows the Democratic nomination, result in a breakdown of public order, the University of Arkansas had been integrated for nine years. Jimmie Davis promised

1

the voters of Louisiana in 1959 that he would go to jail before allowing a Negro to attend classes with whites, and was elected governor on that platform, in a state whose university had been integrated for eight years. A year later when the Louisiana legislature passed a whole string of bizarre bills designed to prevent even the token integration of the New Orleans public schools, four hundred and twenty-five Negroes were attending the New Orleans branch of Louisiana State University.

In the states of the Deep South where no Negroes attended white universities before 1954, the first assault on segregation also came in higher education, but it came after the battle lines were drawn. As a result, it was considered as much of a threat to the system as if it had come in the grade schools or high schools. The Negro students involved had none of the anonymity of those who had integrated the universities of Arkansas, Louisiana, Virginia, North Carolina, and Tennessee; nor were they blurred by inclusion in a group, like the teen-agers in Little Rock or the four first-graders in New Orleans. One after another they became famous, but usually only for two or three weeks. Their names, in most cases, faded so quickly from the news that many people find it hard to keep them straight: Autherine Lucy at the University of Alabama, Charlayne Hunter and Hamilton Holmes at the University of Georgia, James H. Meredith at the University of Mississippi, Harvey Gantt at Clemson College in South Carolina. Student Heroes of a strange new kind, they were famed for no achievements in athletics or scholarship but merely for showing up to attend classes.

Their presence was the test of segregation, whether the test resulted in successful defiance, as in Alabama, where Autherine Lucy was expelled after three days for accusing the university administration of complicity in the riots that accompanied her arrival, or in peaceful compliance, as in South Carolina, where those who control the state decided in advance that upon Harvey Gantt's admission to Clemson order would be self-consciously maintained. Nowhere was the test more decisive than in Georgia, where Charlayne Hunter and Hamilton Holmes, two Negroes from Atlanta, entered the state university, in Athens, in January 1961. During their first week at the university —which began in relative calm, was climaxed by their both being suspended "for their own safety" after a riot, and ended with both returning to the campus under a new court order—Georgia abandoned its policy of all-out resistance and accepted desegregated education.

According to the lawyer for the plaintiffs, an Atlanta Negro named Donald Hollowell, the University of Georgia case was "the case that turned the state around and allowed them to start, or at least to *see,* what was in the other direction." Few would disagree with Hollowell's belief that the enrollment of Charlayne and Hamilton in the university was the turning point for Georgia, and was accomplished in a way and at a time that made it inevitable (a word formerly scorned and now almost popular in Georgia) that the state would move forward rather than backward. The walk out of the Deep South mentality was later accelerated a good deal by a federal court ruling against the County Unit System, which formerly made Georgia the only state to elect not only its legislature but its governors, senators, and congressmen by a voting system designed to favor the rural voter, and when Charlayne and Hamilton graduated from the university in June 1963 the atmosphere in Georgia was far different from what it had been when they showed up in Athens on a cold Monday morning two and a half years before.

Both Charlayne and Hamilton had entered the univer-

sity of Georgia after completing the first half of their
sophomore year elsewhere—Hamilton had gone to Morehouse, a private Negro men's college in Atlanta, and
Charlayne to Wayne University in Detroit during the year
and a half it took them to get into Georgia after first applying for admission—and when they graduated they became the first of the Student Heroes to have completed
their education, or at least their undergraduate education.
As a reporter then based in Atlanta, I had covered both
the week-long trial that resulted in their admission and
the events that followed their arrival on campus in 1961,
and in the spring of 1963, about ten weeks before Charlayne and Hamilton graduated, I returned to Georgia
from New York, where I had been living, to see how integration had worked out at the University of Georgia—
whether or not the Student Heroes had ever become simply students, and how two bright young people happened
to become Student Heroes in the first place.

Both had always been considered perfectly cast for the
role. Good-looking and well dressed, they seemed to be
light-complexioned Negro versions of ideal college students, models for an autumn Coca-Cola ad in a Negro
magazine. Charlayne, a slim, attractive girl with striking
hazel eyes, had finished third in her graduating class at
Turner High School in Atlanta, had edited the school
paper, and had been crowned Miss Turner. The valedictorian at Turner that year was Hamilton, who had been
president of the senior class and, as a smaller than average but effective halfback, co-captain of the football team.
Since Charlayne and Hamilton had been such unlikely
targets for abuse from the start, and had eventually been
joined at the university by several other Negro undergraduates, the situation, looked at from a distance, seemed
rather heartening. None of the stories from Georgia about

school integration had mentioned any violence done to the pioneers. They dealt instead with the peaceful integration of public schools in Atlanta and the admission of Negroes to Georgia Tech in September 1961 without even the pressure of a court case. The atmosphere was such that Emory University, a private school in Atlanta, had been able to desegregate its nursing school voluntarily and was planning the integration of its medical school, having already chosen Hamilton Holmes as its first Negro medical student. But I knew from occasional communications I had had from Charlayne and Hamilton since they entered the university that the general progress of the state of Georgia often did not seem closely related to the problems facing the first Negroes at the University of Georgia day after day. I was reminded of this again by Charlayne's reply to a letter I wrote her announcing my plans to revisit the campus. "Well, this is Brotherhood Week in Athens," she concluded, with characteristic irony, "and I'm going out to stand on the street corner and wait for an invitation to lunch."

2

ATLANTA, called the Dogwood City on the city-limits signs, claims to have the most beautiful spring in America, and on my first day there the claim seemed justified. It was a warm March day, and in the heavily wooded residential sections the white dogwood blossoms were already coming out. Downtown, I saw another rite of spring. Some Negro students—like all students, always more likely to protest in the spring—were picketing the Henry Grady Hotel on Peachtree Street. The pickets, who also included two or three white students, were protesting the white-only policy maintained by the Henry Grady and most other Atlanta hotels. One sign read "No Room at This Inn." Another, more to the point in a city that prides itself on being concerned chiefly with commercial competition, read "Dallas, Houston, and Miami—Why Not Atlanta?" To anyone who had lived in Atlanta in recent

6

years, it was a familiar sight. The students, solemn and
neatly dressed, were walking slowly up and down
Peachtree, careful to stay the correct distance apart. Two
or three Atlanta policemen, assigned to make certain that
the incident could be reported as having resulted in "no
incidents," stood in the shade of the hotel, but few of the
passing shoppers gave the pickets a glance. I had
watched the students picket department stores and movie
theaters in Atlanta two years before, and it occurred to
me that they would have little left to picket after the restaurants and hotels were desegregated—a move that
seemed inevitable. (The word had always had some cur-
rency in Atlanta, even when it was not used in the rest
of the state.) The hotel keepers were already under pressure from businessmen, the editors of the newspapers,
and members of the city administration, all of whom kept
pointing out that hotel segregation might be costing Atlanta millions every year in convention business, plus a
possible World's Fair. The progressive Atlanta *Constitution*, which had only urged reasonable negotiations during previous demonstrations, had just come out flatly for
desegregation of the hotels. Race relations in Atlanta, it
seemed to me during my stay there, had taken on a
faintly Northern flavor, with a lot of talk about brotherhood and the fine relations between the races, and great
satisfaction at having schools that were technically integrated but did not actually have many Negroes in classes
with whites. The last race story I had read about Atlanta
was on an essentially Northern topic—housing. The story,
which concerned the erection of wooden barricades by
the city across two streets between a Negro neighborhood and a white neighborhood that felt itself threatened
by infiltration, even had a Northern ending. A judge of
the state superior court—not a federal judge—ruled that

the roadblocks, which had become nationally known as "Atlanta's Wall," were obviously racial barriers and were therefore unconstitutional. He ordered the blemishes on Atlanta's image removed, whereupon the white home-owners, announcing that they had nothing against Negroes, decided to move out of the neighborhood as a group.

The Atlanta Negro community has traditionally been led by the wealthy businessmen who run the insurance companies, banks, and real-estate offices on Auburn Avenue and by the presidents of the six private Negro colleges that make up Atlanta University Center, and it has long had a considerable middle class whose level of prosperity and education is the highest in the Negro South. Negroes have registered freely since 1944, when the white primary was declared unconstitutional, and in the two mayoral elections in Atlanta preceding my visit the candidate elected mayor did not have a white majority. But even though Atlanta was a relatively enlight-ened city—"too busy to hate," the former mayor used to say—it had desegregated practically no public facilities by the late fifties. The traditional leaders of the Negro community, usually called the Old Leadership, seemed to have settled into the belief that the white businessmen, always called the Power Structure, would take care of everything in time if the boat remained unrocked and the voting coalition remained unbroken.

"Atlanta was comparing itself to Mississippi and saying how enlightened it was," says Whitney Young, Jr., the executive director of the National Urban League and a former dean of the Atlanta University School of Social Work. "Nothing was really integrated, not even the library or the buses, but the people were beginning to believe their own press clippings—even the Negroes." Early

in 1958, to make a study of just what had been done in
Atlanta toward equality for the one out of three citizens
who was a Negro, Young and several other Negroes, most
of whom were in their forties and most of whom had
their headquarters on Hunter Street, in the newer Negro
district, rather than on Auburn Avenue, started an informal group called The Atlanta Committee for Cooperative Action, or A.C.C.A. The editor of the study, which
was published eight months later under the title *A Second Look,* was Carl Holman, who was then an English
professor at Atlanta University Center's Clark College
and later became the public-information officer for the
Civil Rights Commission in Washington, D.C. From 1960
to 1962, Holman was also editor of the Atlanta *Inquirer,*
a lively and militant weekly founded during the Atlanta
sit-ins by him and some other Negroes, most of whom
were members of the same A.C.C.A. group and all of
whom were fed up with the cautious policies of Atlanta's
Negro daily newspaper. By the time *A Second Look* was
published, it had the backing and financial assistance of
the Old Leadership, and it immediately became a guide to
the action that was needed. The younger men, working
through existing organizations whenever that was possible and forming new ones when it wasn't, initiated the
action, pulling the Old Leadership behind them—the pattern that integration activities in Atlanta have followed
ever since. The man from the A.C.C.A. group who was
most concerned with school integration was Jesse Hill,
Jr., the energetic young chief actuary of the Atlanta Life
Insurance Company, which is the second largest life-
insurance company in Georgia and one of Auburn Avenue's most solid institutions.

In 1957, Hill, who was a member of the education committee of the local branch of the National Association for

the Advancement of Colored People, had enlisted the help of two or three other Negro leaders in an attempt to desegregate the Georgia State College of Business Administration in Atlanta. Georgia State had the advantage of being a city college with no dormitories, which obviated travel and rooming problems, and of having night sessions. "In those days," Hill told me when I visited him in Atlanta, "people hesitated to send a seventeen-year old kid into that hostility, and we were working mainly to get older people to try for the night school. Frankly, we did some real campaigning. We tried to get some of the people in our own office, for instance. We got three girls to apply, and we won our court case, although the judge didn't order the plaintiffs admitted. By that time, the state had investigated the girls who were applying and found some illegitimate births and that kind of thing with two, and they would have probably been turned down on so-called moral grounds. Then, the state passed a law that said nobody over twenty-one could start as an undergraduate in a Georgia college, which eliminated the third girl and ended any chance of having older people apply for Georgia State."

In 1958, working quietly (in anti-integration bills passed after the 1954 decision, Georgia strengthened its laws against barratry, or incitement of litigation), Hill and some of the other younger men compiled a list of outstanding seniors in the Atlanta Negro high schools and began to approach those whose academic records were so good that a college would have to find other reasons for rejecting them. Hill talked to about a dozen students. Some of them were considering Georgia State; others were more interested in the University of Georgia or Georgia Tech or the state medical college at Augusta. Ultimately, either because something in their background made them vulnerable to one kind of attack or another, or because of a final unwillingness to go through with it, none of them actually applied. Then, in June 1959, Hill found Charlayne and Hamilton.

"Ordinarily this is a selling job," Hill told me. "You have to go seek out and work with these people and do quite a bit of selling. That's how it's been with the other kids at Georgia and those in the Atlanta schools and all. But not Hamilton and Charlayne. They had an almost normal desire to go to the University of Georgia—as normal as you could expect from a Negro in a segregated community. They both knew something about the school; Hamilton had followed the football team and Charlayne knew all about the journalism school. They were almost like two kids from Northside." Northside is a formerly all-white high school in Atlanta's best residential district, and it may be a sign of progress that one of the Negro freshmen who entered Georgia Tech in 1962 actually *was* from Northside, having gone there as one of the nine Negro seniors who integrated Atlanta high schools in 1961.

"Hamilton Holmes was on the list," Hill went on, "but I really didn't have to recruit those kids; they almost recruited me. They knew just what they wanted. I took them by Georgia State. We were after a breakthrough and we had a good chance there. The judge had retained jurisdiction in the case, and Georgia State had plenty of vacancies because of this age law. The Atlanta *Journal* had run pictures of almost empty classrooms. That was important; after all, the University of Georgia kept Charlayne and Hamilton out for a year just by saying they were overcrowded, and it sounded pretty legitimate on the face of it. Anyway, Charlayne and Hamilton wouldn't hear of going to Georgia State. Both of them wanted to go to Georgia. Why they wanted to go I'll never know, but it happened that that was the right thing. It got straight to the heart of the matter. I think the governor might have closed Georgia State or the Atlanta high schools if they had come first, but Georgia, with all those legislators' sons over there and the way everybody in the state feels about it, was different. He wouldn't dare close it."

Once Charlayne and Hamilton had decided to go to Georgia, Hill set out to do battle again with the system that had defeated him in the Georgia State case. He sent the first volley of letters and phone calls through the facilities of Atlanta Life, and then got the local N.A.A.C.P. branch to put up the money for legal expenses that were necessarily incurred before the litigation got far enough along to be eligible for aid from the N.A.A.C.P. Legal Defense and Educational Fund, Inc. (a separate corporation from the N.A.A.C.P. itself, and usually called The Inc. Fund, or The Ink Fund). Hill called around the country to find the Turner High School principal, whose signature was required on the application forms and who had left for the summer. Hill went to the Fulton County Courthouse with Charlayne and Hamilton, towing their pastors along as references, and was passed from judge to judge until the clerk of the Fulton County Superior Court finally agreed to certify that both of the students were residents of the State of Georgia, documentation that the federal court had ruled was adequate without the addition of alumni recommendations, which were formerly required and which were not easily obtained by Negro applicants. Hill, Holman, and Young met with Charlayne and Hamilton to warn them of what to expect from Georgia admission officials and Georgia students.

"I had sent for application blanks and a catalogue and hadn't got them," said Hill. "We wanted to make sure we had them in time. Like most places, the University of

Georgia has Negroes to do the cleaning up, and one of the janitors got application blanks and catalogues for us. Every time we made a step we double-checked. I must have written a hundred letters to the university; they wouldn't tell you anything. Don Hollowell checked every letter. We had to certify it and send it registered mail, receipt requested. Anything that got lost, that was the end of that for another year. It was just like pulling teeth. Carl Holman checked and double-checked the applications. We didn't leave anything to chance. And still it took a year and a half."

The energy was provided by the same men who had published "A Second Look." In the first weeks after Charlayne and Hamilton applied, the A.C.C.A. group even maintained a nightly patrol of Charlayne's house. (Atlanta has always had more bombings than Southern cities with otherwise less progressive race relations; there were a dozen in the twelve months prior to public-school integration.) Support from the rest of the Negro community varied greatly. Some people thought Georgia Tech or the Atlanta public schools would be a better place to begin. Others believed that it was rather early to begin anywhere. "A lot of people were opposed to this," Hill told me. "They said, 'These people are going to take reprisals on us. There'll be a loss of jobs, and all.' During the Georgia State case, one leader of the Negro community said, 'Why'd you take those unwed mothers over there?' After Charlayne and Hamilton applied at Georgia, he said, 'Why'd you take those two fine kids over there?' All we ever got from the older leaders was 'You're going to mess up some kids.' "

3

Just why "two fine kids" like Hamilton and Charlayne should want to go to any Southern white college is a question often asked in the North, where many people take it for granted that a Negro student would go to jail for the right to eat a dime-store hamburger but must have an elaborate motive for going to a formerly all-white school. Most white Southerners have already settled the question to their own satisfaction. They believe that the students are chosen by the N.A.A.C.P.—hand-picked by one of the crafty operators from New York, where all evil finds its source, and probably paid handsomely for their services. The New York–based N.A.A.C.P. conspiracy remains a strong vision to most white Southerners, even though it should be apparent by now that if the N.A.A.C.P. had a tenth of the resources and efficiency they credit it with, segregation would have been eradicated years ago.

As for Negroes in Atlanta, when they talk about why

Hamilton went to the University of Georgia they usually begin by mentioning his family, and especially his grandfather, Dr. Hamilton Mayo Holmes, who is an Atlanta physician and the family patriarch. Hamilton is not only a third-generation college graduate; he is also a third-generation integrationist. His grandfather, his father, and one of his uncles filed suit to desegregate the Atlanta public golf courses in 1955, and, through a 1956 Supreme Court decision on their case, the courses became the first integrated public facility in Atlanta. I had spent some time with Hamilton's father, Alfred Holmes, during the integration in Athens, and on one of the first days of my return visit to Atlanta I arranged to talk with him at his office about both his son and his father. Alfred Holmes, who is known in Atlanta as Tup, is a short, chunky man with a breezy manner and a cheerful, chipmunkish expression. He seems to know everybody on the street, whether it is Hunter Street or Auburn Avenue in Atlanta or Hancock Avenue in Athens, where he worked for six or eight months as an embalmer early in his career. Almost everybody he sees gets a cheery "How you makin' it?" or "You makin' it okay?" Strictly Hunter Street in philosophy himself, Tup Holmes shares an office building there with the Atlanta *Inquirer*, the law offices of Donald Hollowell and associates, the local branch of the N.A.A.C.P. (which had disturbed some of the Old Leadership by moving there from Auburn Avenue not long before), the Southeastern Regional Office of the N.A.A.C.P., and a school for beauticians. Holmes has been in several businesses, mostly selling one thing or another, and the small office he ushered me into was devoted to the sale of real estate and insurance. Having assured him that I was making it okay, I asked Holmes about Hamilton's decision to go to the University of Georgia.

"The aggressiveness of the family might have influenced him, but Hamp's a steady sort of boy," Holmes said. "He's always thought deeply and on his own. Jesse Hill asked if I would mention Georgia to Hamp, because he was just about perfect, with his grades and his personality. That's all I had to do was mention it; before I could do anything else he had already talked to Jesse. I went down to Athens once or twice, and I tell you he's two different people when he's there and when he's in Atlanta. He lives for Friday afternoon, when he can come home. There's really no one in that town for him to talk to, and he's not the kind to do much visiting. He sticks to his lessons. He made up his mind he was going to make those crackers sit up and take notice. You know, I travel around the state quite a bit in my business, and sometimes I talk in the high schools or the churches. I didn't realize for quite a while what a hero this boy is to those people in the backwoods. When I'm being introduced to a group of people, sooner or later the man introducing me gets around to saying, 'This is the father of Hamilton Holmes.' And they say, 'You mean the Hamilton Holmes up at Georgia? Let me shake your hand.' I think he means so much to those people because of his grades. The white man in the South has always accepted the Negro as his equal or superior physically, because he figures we're not far removed from the jungle and we've had to do physical work for so long that our muscles have got hard. But the whites never have accepted us as their equal or superior mentally. They have always said that the Negro is only good for plowing. Well, Hamp is destroying all those myths. He's made the Phi Kappa Phi honor society, you know, and we hope he'll make Phi Beta Kappa. When those people in the backwoods see those A's, they stand up. That's why he means more to them than James Meredith, or even Charlayne."

After we had talked a while longer, Holmes said, "Well, if you're going to get in to see Daddy we better get over there. If you come after eleven-thirty, there's so many patients you can't get near the place." On the drive from Hunter Street to Auburn Avenue, where Dr. Holmes has his office, Tup Holmes told me about his father, whose prowess as a doctor, a golfer, and a speaker makes him almost as popular a subject for conversation in the Holmes family as Hamilton. "My daddy's a real scrapper," Tup Holmes said. "He ran away from home when he was twelve to go to school. He was from Louisiana. The backwoods—and I mean the real backwoods. He worked in the sugar mills in New Orleans and went to school at night in a small school that's now part of Dillard. Then he worked his way through Shaw Medical School, in North Carolina, and came to Atlanta to practice—in 1910. He's a real scrapper. Daddy was a pioneer on this golf-course thing. It required a lot of courage on his part, especially considering all the training and inhibitions of his generation. You have to remember that when he was coming up he would have to tip his hat and move to the side every time he saw a white lady on the street."

When we arrived at Dr. Holmes' office, on the fourth floor of an old building on Auburn Avenue, it was half an hour before his office hours began, but six or eight patients were already sitting in the plain waiting room, watching television. They hardly looked up as Holmes and I walked into the doctor's office, where a nurse from the adjoining treatment room told us to make ourselves comfortable until the doctor arrived. Dr. Holmes' office was a small room containing an old-fashioned desk, a refrigerator, a daybed, a floor safe with a filing cabinet on top of it, and two or three tables. Almost every flat surface was covered with golfing trophies, and the walls were covered with a staggering collection of plaques, pictures, and framed prayers. There were several religious pictures, some family pictures, and numerous plaques from golf organizations and fraternities. In one frame were three glossy prints of Hamilton and Charlayne and a letter from the Half Century Alumni Club of Shaw University. The wall decorations also included a chart showing the postal zone of every street in Atlanta, a sports award from radio station WSB for a hole-in-one made on January 1, 1961, and a cardboard reprint of the Prayer for Physicians by Maimonides. Between a plaque signifying life membership in the United Golfers Association, which is the Negro equivalent of the U.S. Golfers Association, and a poem about medicine from the Fifty Year Club of American Medicine hung an eye chart.

After a few minutes Dr. Holmes bustled in. A jolly man, shorter, chunkier, and darker than his progeny, he had a tiny gray moustache and a tiny gray goatee. Since he also had tufts of gray hair on the sides of his head and more tufts of gray hair for eyebrows, he looked like a tiny Uncle Remus. He wore a three-piece blue suit, a diamond stickpin, and a watch chain. When Dr. Holmes heard I was there to ask about Hamilton, he could hardly wait to begin.

"I trained my children from infancy to fear nothing, and I told my grandson the same thing," Dr. Holmes said. "I told him to be meek. Be meek, but don't look too humble. Because if you look too humble they might think you're afraid, and there's nothing to be afraid about, because the Lord will send his angel to watch over you and you have nothing to fear. I'm glad Hamp has faith; you have to have faith. Science is not enough; you have to have more than science. You have to know the Lord is watching over you. Hamp is a religious boy and he's a natural-born doctor. He's wanted to be a doctor since infancy. I told his mother before he was born, I said, 'You just think on medicine and if it's a boy maybe the prenatal influence will make him a natural-born doctor.' And she did think on it, and sure enough, that's what he is, a natural-born doctor."

Dr. Holmes talked a bit about his own practice. "I've been practicing medicine here for fifty-three years," he said, "and I'm busier now than I've ever been. I come in at eleven-forty-five and I stay until four-thirty or five. I come back at seven and stay till ten-thirty or eleven. I don't much like to work past eleven any more. I try to treat everybody as an individual. Once, a lady came in and said, 'You sure took a long time with that last patient,' and I said, 'Okay, if you want I'll hurry on you.' She said, 'Don't hurry on me. Oh, no!' Well, I treat them all like individuals, but I still see fifty or sixty patients a day. I work every day but Wednesday and Sunday. I play golf on Wednesdays, and on Sundays I go to church. Then I play golf."

I asked Dr. Holmes if his game was still as good as the trophies indicated. "I beat nearly everybody I play with, young and old alike," he admitted. "They say, 'I'm waiting for you to get tired.' I tell them they better beat me now because I'm not going to get tired. I'll be seventy-nine on the fourth of April, but not an ache, not a pain, not a stiffness in the joints. Not a corn, not a callus, not a bunion on my feet. And my memory is as good as it was fifty years ago."

Dr. Holmes stretched his muscles and his joints to demonstrate their efficiency. I had no reason to doubt it, or to doubt his memory.

"Hamp's granddaddy is quite a character," Charlayne told me a day or two later. "He called up once and said he'd decided Hamp and I should get married, and he'd give me any kind of convertible I wanted for a wedding present. He hadn't consulted Hamp, of course. I explained to him that Hamp and I were more like brother and sister, and that Hamp had a girl. But he said we would just have to get married because we'd have such smart children."

Charlayne, unlike Hamilton, is rarely explained as the logical result of a family tradition. In fact, even at the age of eighteen, when she entered the University of Georgia, she seemed remarkably independent. "She's always wanted to be out front," I was once told by her mother, a pretty, retiring woman who works as a secretary in a Negro real-estate company. "When she was a little girl I never had to get after her to do her lessons or anything. She's just always been that way." Charlayne's poise during the first days of integration was occasionally attributed to her having spent her eighth-grade year as one of only a few Negroes in an integrated Army school in Alaska, where her father, a career Army chaplain, was stationed. Charles Hunter, who retired with the rank of lieutenant colonel while Charlayne was in college, was often the first Negro to hold whatever post he was assigned to, but the extent of his influence on Charlayne is not certain. He and Mrs. Hunter separated after the year in Alaska, and Charlayne, who had previously gone for long stretches without seeing her father while he was overseas, rarely saw him after she returned to Atlanta to live with her mother, her two younger brothers, and her grandmother. Charlayne's father is a Methodist minister, and her mother is also a Methodist, but Charlayne became a Catholic when she was sixteen.

At Georgia, Charlayne continued to look at things from a point of view of her own, and, because she was a journalism student, she had a kind of double vision for two and a half years. During her first hectic week or two at Georgia, she sometimes seemed to be watching the reporters watch her integrate the university, occasionally making notes on both phenomena for an article in the Atlanta *Inquirer*. According to Carl Holman, who, as editor of the *Inquirer*, had also found that covering the integration news often meant observing his own activities, "It gave her a detachment she might not have had otherwise. Hamilton has the views of the average citizen on the subject; that is, he regards reporters as just as dangerous as anyone else. But Charlayne was always studying them, and I think it made her feel better that they were around."

One day during my return visit to Atlanta, while Charlayne was at home for several days after her next-to-last round of final examinations at Georgia, she and I met for lunch at a restaurant on Hunter Street, and I found that she was still able to see her experience as a news story. Although she had always received more attention in the press than Hamilton, she assured me that Hamilton made a better study. "He's consistent and I'm not," she said. "He knows what he wants and where he's going and how he's going to get there. We're a lot different. For instance, he can't wait for Friday. He comes back to Atlanta every week end. He has a girl here, and his family. I think my mother and brothers are great, but that's the only reason I come home at all. I'd just as soon stay in Athens and sleep or read. Hamp's very uncomfortable there. For one thing, he's not crazy about white people. And he loves Atlanta. I guess I'm just as comfortable there as I am anyplace else.

"Hamp and I were sort of rivals at Turner, but we usually agreed on big things. I wanted to go to journalism school, and I had considered Georgia, but not really seriously. It seemed such a remote possibility. I had just about decided to go to Wayne, for no special reason except they had a journalism school and had answered my letters and I wanted to go to school away from home. When Hamp brought up Georgia—I think it was while we were posing together for a yearbook picture—I said sure, I'd like to go. It seemed like a good idea. I can't stress enough that I didn't ponder it. I guess it always was in my mind that I had the right, but Hamp and I never had any discussions about Unalienable, God-given Rights. We just didn't speak in those terms. It sounded like an interesting thing to do, and in the back of my mind I kept thinking this would never really happen; it was just something we were doing. I guess at that stage of the game we thought that anything we wanted to do was possible. Each step got us more involved, but we didn't think of it that way. We just went step by step, and it seemed kind of like a dream. When we got together with Jesse Hill and Hollowell and Carl and Whitney Young, they thought we ought to go to Georgia State. It also had journalism courses, and I really didn't know the difference. Negro kids don't know anything about white colleges. We figured if it was white it was good. We picked up applications at Georgia State, but neither one of us really liked the place; the catalogue showed they really didn't offer much. We went out on the steps and stood around, and Hamp said, 'I want to go to Athens. That's the place to go.' And he pointed right in the direction of Athens. I said 'I'm with you,' and they said 'Okay, you'll go to Athens.' I think a lot of it was Hamp's having always taken an interest in the Georgia football team."

One reason for the dreamlike quality of the eighteen months that followed was that, except for two or three hearings they had to attend, Charlayne and Hamilton were merely spectators of the complicated maneuvers that Jesse Hill and Donald Hollowell—eventually joined by Constance Baker Motley, associate counsel of the Inc. Fund—were carrying on with the state. Charlayne and Hamilton each submitted a continuing application, which was regularly turned down, usually on the ground of a space shortage, and all they had to do to be rejected again was submit their college transcripts each semester. They did have to appear in federal district court in Macon, in the summer between their freshman and sophomore years. At that time Judge William Bootle refused to order them into the university through a temporary restraining order, ruling that they had not exhausted their administrative remedies, but he did schedule a December trial on a motion for a permanent injunction. Under Judge Bootle's orders, Charlayne and Hamilton both went to Athens that November for admission interviews, at which Charlayne was treated politely and Hamilton, appearing before a three-man panel, was asked such questions as whether or not he had ever been to a house of prostitution or a "tea parlor" or "beatnik places"—questions that, Bootle later noted in judicial understatement, "had probably never been asked of any applicant before."

All-out stalling is not an ineffective strategy, as Southern white strategies against integration go. It worked well against the first Negro who tried to get into the University of Georgia—Horace Ward, who sued for admission to the law school in 1952. The stalling went on until 1957, by which time Ward had stayed out of school for a year or so, had then been drafted, had served in the Army, and had finally entered another law school, so that a federal judge ruled the case moot. The possibilities of carefully managed stalling are demonstrated in a sentence from the decision that eventually ordered the university to admit

Charlayne and Hamilton. "Plaintiffs have already prose-
cuted one appeal through administrative channels which
required 122 days for final administrative action," Judge
Bootle wrote. "If plaintiffs were required to appeal from
defendants' failure to admit them each quarter for which
they made application for admission, they would probably
use up the normal four-year college attendance period before securing any final administrative action." Some federal judges in the South, as a matter of fact, probably
would never have ended the stalling, since the reasons
given for rejecting Charlayne and Hamilton always
sounded plausible enough.

And such delaying tactics, even if it could be assumed
that they would end sooner or later, force applicants either
to stay out of school, which Charlayne and Hamilton, am-
bitious and anxious to get started, would obviously not
do, or to enter another college and complicate their
problems by applying as transfer students. Georgia admission officials said they were very much concerned about
the credits Charlayne and Hamilton might lose if they
transferred in the middle of the year from colleges that
divide the school year into two semesters to a college that,
like the University of Georgia, divides it into three quarters (the summer session constitutes the fourth quarter).
Shortly after Charlayne and Hamilton applied, Georgia
began to accept transfer students only when they fell into
certain categories, supposedly based on whether a transfer was necessary for the continuation of a student's program, and Charlayne never seemed to be in the right
category.

Also, after a year and a half of college life among
friends, facing the hostility of the University of Georgia
seemed much less appealing to both students than it had
seemed following high-school graduation, when Georgia

had sounded like a good idea and like something a long way off. This was especially true of Hamilton, who went to Morehouse, the most highly regarded of the Atlanta University Center colleges. An alumnus of Morehouse—Charlayne's father is one—is always called a "Morehouse man" by Atlanta Negroes, who are proud of A.U.'s School of Social Work, and of Spelman, its girls' college, but especially of Morehouse. During a visit to see Hamilton's mother while I was back in Atlanta, I asked his brother Herbert, a freshman at Morehouse, how he thought Hamilton compared Morehouse and Georgia, and I was assured that Hamilton preferred Morehouse in every respect but one: he thought Georgia's science facilities were superior. Herbert seemed concerned lest I get the impression that anybody could be happier anywhere than he could be at Morehouse.

The mantelpiece of the Holmes house had almost as many trophies for Hamilton's achievements as a regular student at Morehouse and Turner as for his being a Student Hero at Georgia. I noticed a trophy he had received for being the outstanding freshman football player at Morehouse; a Turner High valedictorian trophy; the National Newspaper Publishers Association Russwurm Award for "making possible a richer conception of democratic principles"; a trophy from Turner for excellence in math; two trophies for his attendance at Georgia from Alpha Phi Alpha, the fraternity Hamilton joined at Morehouse; and a plaque from the Turner High School P.-T.A. given to Mr. and Mrs. Holmes.

Hamilton's mother, Isabella Holmes, turned out to be an articulate, attractive woman with a gentle voice, which added force to rather than detracted from what she said. She had grown up in Tuskegee, Alabama, where her father edited one of the trade magazines published by Tus-

kegee Institute, and where she met her husband while
both were students at the institute. When Mrs. Holmes
mentions integration she is almost always talking about
the integration of blind and partially sighted children
into regular classrooms—a pioneer program in Atlanta
that Mrs. Holmes, as a sixth-grade teacher, has been taking part in for several years.

"Hamp was supposed to go to Morehouse through the
early admissions program the year before he got out of
Turner," Mrs. Holmes told me. "He had a four-year Mer-
rill Scholarship that paid full tuition. But that summer he
decided he didn't want to give up his senior year at
Turner, and later he decided on Georgia. Then, I remember the day the judge's decision was handed down, after
Hamp had been at Morehouse a year and a half. I saw
that the judge said they didn't have to enter that quarter,
or even spring quarter. And, since I knew how much
Morehouse meant to Hamp, the first thing I said was that
he wouldn't be letting anybody down if he waited until
fall. It surprised me. He said, 'No, I've got to go now.'
Hamp doesn't do much talking, and sometimes you don't
know what he's thinking. It's lonely for him down in
Athens. It's particularly hard for a boy who's from a large
family. With four others, there's no such thing as isolation in this house. You'd think some students there would
make overtures to a boy in a situation like that. It's hard
for me to believe that nobody would bother, unless the boy
was objectionable. I guess I'll never understand. He got so
low last spring, when he saw the other boys playing base-
ball on the lawn and all, that I wanted him to come home
for a while. He wouldn't hear of coming home. If Corky
King, the Presbyterian minister there, hadn't started having him over to dinner every week, I don't know what
would have become of him. I sometimes wish one of my

other boys, Gary, the one who's in college in Charlotte now, had gone instead of Hamp. They could have run him over with a truck and not bothered him. But Hamp is very sensitive in many ways."

I asked Mrs. Holmes how much harassment the family had been subjected to in Atlanta after Hamilton applied. "We had quite a time here with the phone," she said. "I think they had the phone tapped, because they cut in on conversations, and if you left it off the hook it would cut off and go dead and you couldn't call out. We complained to the phone company, and they gave us a private number, but before I even knew the number myself—they sent it by mail—the calls began coming in on that one. They would start about the time I got in from work and go through the night. Sometimes, when we left the phone off the hook, we'd have to cover it with something, because they would just keep talking. And I hated to be without the phone. And I was afraid about somebody passing by. I think I even imagined things when I got into the car and put my foot on the starter. I wondered about jeopardizing other people if somebody passed by and threw something. I did wonder sometimes if it was worth it."

Hamilton spent most of his final spring break filling speaking engagements, a function he had left pretty much to Charlayne during their first two years at Georgia. "I'm getting around a little more," he said, when I finally got him on the phone late that week. "But with me the studies still come first." He went on to say that he was scheduled to speak at the Emmanuel Baptist Church in Atlanta that Sunday, and I arranged to meet the Holmes family there.

Sunday was another beautiful spring day in Atlanta. It

was, in fact, Safe Boating Sunday in WSB-land, the radio announcer said as I drove over to Emmanuel Baptist, a neat, new red-brick church in the middle of a red-brick Negro housing project in the southeastern section of the city. Hamilton's father was chatting with friends in the vestibule when I arrived, and he led me down to the first row, where his wife and his father were already seated. Dr. Holmes looked as natty as he had in his office, wearing a blue suit with a light pin stripe, a blue tie, his diamond stickpin and, hanging from his watch chain, a medallion, which, he told me a few minutes later, was one of Tup's golf awards. "I have a lot of them of my own, but I like this one," he explained. "It looks like a gold dollar. Tup got it in Chicago in 1940 or 1941."

That was enough to turn the conversation to golf.

"About the only time I leave town is for golf tournaments," said Dr. Holmes. "I used to go to a lot of medical meetings, but I'm getting tired of them. I play in three tournaments a year, usually—United Golfers Association tournaments, in the senior division. I usually shoot in the low eighties."

"He kills those old men," Tup Holmes said proudly. "He just kills them. But he hasn't been able to shoot his age yet. It's all mental. He gets a thirty-six or thirty-seven on the first nine and then he gets to thinking about it and he blows it on the back nine. He gets nervous."

Dr. Holmes acknowledged that Tup was the best golfer in the family when he was in form—he won the national U.G.A. in 1947, in Philadelphia, and again in 1958, in Pittsburgh—but said he was able to beat him occasionally. "In the seniors, I win first place sometimes, second place sometimes, and sometimes third place, although not often," he went on. "The seniors are for men over fifty, and you have to remember that I didn't have a golf club in my hand until I was fifty. Some of those other fellows are experienced."

I reminded Dr. Holmes that even though he had a late start, he'd had twenty-nine years of experience. He just smiled and turned toward the pulpit, where the service was about to begin.

According to our programs, the church was holding its Annual Youth Day Observance, on the theme of "Christian Youth and Their Spiritual Challenge in an Emerging Age of World Freedom," although the bulletin board on the lawn outside had said merely, "9:30—Sunday School. 10:45—Hamilton Holmes." About half an hour after the service was scheduled to begin, Hamilton walked on the platform with four girls. He looked about the same as when I had last seen him, almost two years before, except that some extra weight accented the characteristic Holmes heaviness around the jaw. He was, as usual, well dressed, wearing an Ivy League-cut blue summer-weight suit, a rep tie, and a white button-down shirt, and he had a tiny Alpha Phi Alpha pin in his lapel. As Hamilton shifted in his seat through the first part of the service, his face had the serious look that most people at Georgia had interpreted as a scowl. The service, conducted by the four girls, proceeded through an opening hymn, a responsive reading, the morning hymn, a scripture lesson, the morning prayer, a selection by the youth choir, a statement of purpose, several selections by the Turner High School choral ensemble, the collection, and the doxology. Finally one of the girls introduced Hamilton, calling him "a militant and pioneering young speaker who has symbolized and portrayed in his own actions and character the fight for human dignity and first-class citizenship." There was one more hymn, and then Hamilton rose to speak.

Putting on a pair of horn-rimmed glasses, he read from
a prepared text entitled "Higher Education and the New
Negro"—Hamilton's favorite speech topic. He began by
outlining advances in science, in industry, and even in
household labor—advances that had eliminated many
traditional Negro jobs. There was, he went on, an in-
creasing need for highly trained workers, and that need
could be filled by the New Negro, "who realizes he is just
as good as any other man . . . not the Negro sitting pas-
sively around waiting for his rights to be handed to him
on a silver platter." Hamilton said that such movements
as the sit-ins had opened doors but that the Negro must
be prepared to go through them, and that his greatest
drawback was his lack of education.

"Ours is a competitive society," he continued. "This is
true even more so for the Negro. He must compete not
only with other Negroes but with the white man. In most
instances, in competition for jobs and status with whites,
the Negro must have more training and be more qualified than his white counterpart if he is to beat him out of
a job. If the training and qualifications are equal, nine
times out of ten the job will go to the white man. This is a
challenge to us as a race. We must not be content to be
equal, education- and training-wise, but we must strive
to be superior in order to be given an equal chance. This
is something that I have experienced in my short tenure
at the University of Georgia. I cannot feel satisfied with
just equaling the average grades there. I am striving to
be superior. I have found that I *must* be superior in order
to be accepted as an equal. If the average is B, then I
want an A. The importance of superior training cannot be
overemphasized. This is a peculiar situation, I know, but
it is reality, and reality is something that we Negroes
must learn to live with."

That was, I thought, a pretty good summary of Hamilton's philosophy at Georgia—what his father would call "making those crackers sit up and take notice." As Hamilton sat down, a man in the congregation said, in a sonorous voice, "Richly spoken, richly spoken." He turned out to be the minister of Emmanuel Baptist, Benjamin Weldon Bickers, and he came forward at that point to take over from the girls and introduce some guests, including three students from integrated Atlanta high schools. He also introduced Mr. and Mrs. Holmes, and Hamilton's sister, Emma, who had joined the family after singing in the Turner chorus, and two or three more Holmeses, and then somebody reminded him that he had neglected Dr. Holmes. Mr. Bickers not only introduced the doctor but asked him to say a few words.

Dr. Holmes, still beaming over Hamilton's speech, popped right up and turned around to face the congregation. "Brothers and sisters," he said, "I assure you that it is a pleasure to be here. I always hoped I would be able to live long enough to see this young man stand as he stands in the community and in his daily deportment. It gives me a thrill, and I thank the Lord I lived long enough to see it. And to have such a *fine* boy! He does not smoke or chew; he does not drink beer, wine, or liquor. I told him when he was a little boy, 'Never live long enough to smoke or drink.' As a result, here he is. It did me good to hear him philosophize, to go step by step through what the New Negro needs. It did me good, and I thank the Lord I lived long enough to hear him."

The congregation was already nodding in approval as Dr. Holmes digressed briefly to talk about another grandchild, a girl who had gone to Elmira College, in upstate New York, as an exchange student from Spelman and had immediately become the star of the choir. "I'm glad I

took the Biblical advice not to let your riches pile up
where thieves and robbers can get them but to deposit
them in your children," Dr. Holmes went on. "I'm proud of
this boy. And we don't want him to stop. We want him to
get his M.D. or his Ph.D. or whatever D. he wants. He
might be too smart to practice. He might have to teach.
But we want him to have everything he wants. It's a
pleasure to be here."

As Dr. Holmes turned and sat down, there was the
shuffling and murmuring of a congregation that wanted
to show approval but knew better than to clap in church.
Just as I thought I might have witnessed my first Negro
church meeting in the South that had only one collection,
Mr. Bickers announced that he was going to collect Hamilton's honorarium right there, and he passed the plate
again.

Although Hamilton's family has long been active in
community affairs, the only one of his relatives profes-
sionally involved in race relations is his uncle, Oliver
Wendell Holmes, who was destined by Dr. Holmes to be
the family lawyer but ended up as a Congregationalist
minister instead. A small, cheerful man, and the most
direct heir to the patriarch's jolly eloquence, Oliver
Holmes is the associate director of the Georgia Council
on Human Relations. In 1956 the council grew out of the
Georgia Interracial Committee, which was founded right
after the First World War to start some communication
between whites and Negroes, meeting as equals. Among
the early participants in the Georgia Interracial Committee was Oliver Holmes' mother—Hamilton's grandmother
—who, as one of the first Negro registered nurses in the
South, was, before her death, a prominent member of the
Negro community. "Mama used to go have her tea and

cookies once a month," Oliver Holmes recalled when I visited him at the organization's headquarters in Atlanta. "And we'd say, 'Well, mama, you've had your tea and cookies now, and next month you can go have your tea and cookies again.' But I think it actually did do some good. It kept the lines of communication open, and they could have closed easily in those days."

I had first met Oliver Holmes two years before in Savannah, where he had become pastor of the First Congregational Church in 1959, after several years of preaching in Talladega, Alabama. While he was in Talladega, Holmes had organized the area's first N.A.A.C.P. branch, but, he said, the most important case was a criminal one rather than one involving civil rights. It came up when "a drunken Negro cab driver, in a one-eyed car with no brakes, in the rain, hit and killed two white policemen who were harassing a couple of college kids who were parked there by the side of the road doing a little light necking." Holmes went to Birmingham and came back with a young Negro defense lawyer. "They said if a colored lawyer came there to defend that boy he'd be lucky not to get the chair himself," said Holmes. As the case turned out, the cab driver got only five years for manslaughter, because the policemen had been on the wrong side of the road and the accident was, despite his condition and the multiple handicaps of his car, not his fault. "Everybody in the town was just as happy as could be," Holmes told me. "The Negroes said, 'Our lawyer got that boy off with five years' and the whites said, 'Despite that little nigger we put that boy away for five years.' When it came time that he was eligible for parole, we went up to see him at the state prison farm and he said, 'Don't you bother me about any parole. I'm driving a tractor and I got more money in my pocket than I ever had and I don't want to leave. When my time

is up, I'm going to ask for an extension.' Yes sir, *everybody* was happy about that case."

While Holmes was in Talladega, he found time to make
trips to Atlanta for golf, and was in the foursome that
tested the segregation of the public golf course in 1955.
"When we first went out there to make the test they
were a little surprised," he said. "I went up to the window
and asked for four tickets and the man said, 'Tickets for
what?' I told him, 'For whatever you're selling them for.'
And he said he couldn't sell us any tickets because the
course wasn't open to Negroes. I told him that's what I
thought—just testing. After the Supreme Court decision,
we went out to play, and we figured somebody had better
stay home in case something happened. So we finally convinced Daddy that as long as he held the purse strings,
maybe he'd better stay home. He didn't want to. He sure
is crazy about golf, and he was just as excited as he
could be about this. My brother Tup was really up for this
game, with the press out there and everything. I think he
had been practicing for it; he shot a thirty-eight on the
first nine. I had been stuck out in Talladega without much
chance to play and my game was a little off, and maybe I
was a little nervous."

When Holmes moved to Savannah, he found that the
public golf course was available to Negroes only one day
a week, and then did not permit them access to such facilities as the rest rooms and the snack bar. Those were
conditions that would put any Holmes off his game, so
Oliver Holmes worked out a plan with the mayor whereby
the course was at first open to Negroes two days a week,
with the use of all facilities, and then, a couple of months
later, was desegregated completely. The golf-course desegregation worked out so smoothly that the mayor appointed Holmes to the Park Board, which put him in a

good position to work on the integration of the parks. While he was in Savannah, Holmes also worked with the mayor to get the library quietly desegregated and headed the N.A.A.C.P. negotiations committee that, with the aid of a year-long boycott, effected the desegregation of the lunch counters in downtown Savannah department stores. When a human-relations council was formed in Savannah, Holmes was the logical choice for cochairman. "We usually try to have cochairmen, to insure the participation of both races," he told me. "It's always easy to find a Negro cochairman but sometimes not a white. So I was the co-cochairman for a while." Holmes eventually decided to leave the pulpit for a full-time job with the Georgia Council, which, he said, "does a little trouble shooting around the state. We try to see if we can't get the whites and Negroes to sit down and talk. We try to stress reason rather than force."

When I visited Holmes in Atlanta, he had just returned from a little trouble shooting at Jekyll Island, a state-owned resort whose facilities Negroes believed to be not only separate but distinctly unequal. "They have a sign up at the Negro end saying 'Site of Proposed Golf Course,' " Holmes said. "They've been proposing that golf course for three years now. The first time I tried the white golf course, they put out a sign, 'Closed for Watering.' I never heard of a course being closed for watering. You just turn on a hose and water it. Finally they said they did not allow Negroes to use the course." Holmes had then started appearing before the State Park Commission to argue for the desegregation of Jekyll Island. "I saw the Director of State Parks at this hearing," Holmes went on. "He said he lived down in Albany and he asked me, 'With all this trouble down there how do you explain it that I've got a hundred and sixty Negroes working for me, and they're just as happy as they can be. They tell me so.' I explained it. I said 'You got yourself a hundred and sixty of the biggest liars in the state of Georgia.' "

Holmes said that the rest of the Holmes family had always been active in civil rights in one way or another. "My father has always been active in the N.A.A.C.P. in a financial way," he told me. "He's never had time for any other. Of course, since he met golf, he's never had time for much of anything. Hamp's daddy always thought he was entitled to what other people were entitled to, and, unlike some Negroes, he always spoke out. In fact, he always shouted it from the rooftops." Oliver Holmes had arranged for Hamilton to make a speech to the Savannah Human Relations Council the week end before and had gone along to introduce him. When I told him that I had heard Hamilton speak at Emmanuel Church, and had unexpectedly heard a speech from Dr. Holmes as well, Holmes laughed and said, "I've been asked to preach twice since I left the ministry, and both times I took my daddy with me. Both times they asked him to say a few words after the sermon, and both times he gave a better speech than I did. He really killed me. The second time, the fellow behind me said right out loud, so I could hear, 'That's the one who should be preaching.' I told Daddy next time I got an invitation I wasn't going to tell him about it. When I heard that he spoke in church where Hamp spoke, I said, 'I hope he didn't kill Hamp like he killed me.' "

4

ALTHOUGH Hamilton's high-school record indicated that
he was likely to have an outstanding academic career at
Georgia, he was found unqualified before he went to
court, and not, said the officials, because he was a Negro.
Shortly before the trial in Athens federal court in December 1960, at which I first met Charlayne and Hamilton,
the university registrar and director of admissions, Walter
Danner, having considered the interviews with both students, wrote Charlayne that she would be considered
for admission the following fall—there was no room for
transfer students in her category before then—and wrote
Hamilton that he had been rejected on the basis of his interview. Hamilton, the Registrar said, had been "evasive"
in answering the questions put to him by the three-man
panel, and had left its members in "some doubt as to his
truthfulness." As Hollowell later brought out in the trial,

37

these were almost exactly the same reasons a special in-
terviewing board had given eight years before for decid-
ing that Horace Ward was unqualified to be a lawyer and
should therefore be rejected by the University of Georgia
Law School. (Ward had gone on to Northwestern Law
School, had returned to join Hollowell's office in Atlanta,
and must have derived a good deal of satisfaction from
assisting Hollowell and Mrs. Motley in the trial, not to
mention escorting Hamilton into the admissions office to
register a month later.) The charge of untruthfulness
was based on Hamilton's having given a negative reply to
the board's question of whether or not he had ever been
arrested. The admissions office, Danner said in court, just
happened to know that Hamilton had once been fined
and had had his license suspended for speeding, and the
office considered that an arrest.

Before the trial, Mrs. Motley and three assistants spent
two weeks going through the Georgia admission files,
which had been opened by court order. By comparing the
treatment given Charlayne and Hamilton with that given
other students, they had no difficulty in demonstrating
that the whole business was a subterfuge, that the only
real category the university had was white, and that the
interviewers were less interested in Hamilton's speeding
ticket than in the impossibility of stalling him any longer
by claiming that the dormitories were overcrowded, since
university rules permitted male students to live off campus after their freshman year. The housing problem was
not so acute that the university had to refrain from sending an agriculture dean to upstate New York that year to
recruit students for its food-technology program. And the
interview that had been considered so important in Hamilton's case was given to some students *after* they were
already attending the University.

The University, of course, had been double-dealing for a year and a half, and it was instructive to see the double-dealing presented as a legal defense by a state that had vowed open resistance to integration. In the effort to correct the false notion that the South has a monopoly on bigotry, the equally false notion has been created that the North has a monopoly on hypocrisy, and I had often heard it said that "in the South at least everybody knows where he stands and people are honest about it." According to this way of thinking, the resistance promised on the campaign stump by politicians should have been continued in court by state officials. But the university officials I listened to for a week in Athens, testifying about their overcrowded dormitories and their administrative problems, sounded less like Southerners fighting a holy crusade than like Long Island real-estate brokers trying to wriggle out of an anti-discrimination law. After one has spent a few minutes listening to a desegregation trial, the reason for this shift becomes clear. It is a simple matter of law. In federal court, where the case must be tried, the issue has already been decided: segregation in the public schools is unconstitutional. The only possible defense is that segregation does not exist. When politicians say they will resist integration "by all legal means," they can mean only that they will try to prolong litigation by any available dodge, since the issue has already been settled by all legal means. In Georgia, in 1960, a trial had to be held. It was demanded by what had evolved into a ritual of combating integration even when it was obvious that the combat would do no good.

In a state whose highest officials were declaring daily that there would be no integration, a state that had a law on the books establishing that funds would be cut off from any school that was integrated, a state whose governor had promised in his campaign that "not one, no, not one" Negro would ever attend classes with whites in Georgia, Omer Clyde Aderhold, the president of the University of Georgia, had the following exchange with the state's own lawyer, B. D. Murphy:

MURPHY: Now I'll ask you if, as an official of the University of Georgia for the period you have stated and as President of the University of Georgia since 1950, do you know of any policy of the University of Georgia to exclude students on account of their race or color?

ADERHOLD: No sir, I do not.

MURPHY: Do you know of any policy to discriminate against Negro applicants?

ADERHOLD: I do not.

MURPHY: Have you ever had any instructions from the Chancellor of the University System or the Chairman of the Board of Regents or anybody else to exclude Negroes as applicants to the University of Georgia?

ADERHOLD: I have not.

MURPHY: Have their applications, so far as you know, been considered on the same basis as the applications of white people?

ADERHOLD: On exactly the same basis, as far as I know.

The Chancellor of the University System, which is composed of all the public colleges and universities in the state, was Harmon W. Caldwell, a respected former president of the University of Georgia. He had sworn in the Horace Ward trial that he would recommend admission of a qualified Negro, and now he had to read in court a note he had sent to Aderhold on that subject. The note, attached to a letter requesting Caldwell to use his influence to get a white girl into the university, had been found in the admission files by one of Mrs. Motley's assistants. It read, "I have written Howard [Howard Callaway, a member of the Board of Regents] that it is my understanding that all of the dormitories for women are filled for the coming year. I have also indicated that you relied on this fact to bar the admission of a Negro girl from Atlanta. . . ."

Although the spectacle of Aderhold and Caldwell in court was a particularly sad example of what the Ritual can lead to, it was by no means unusual. In one brief, Georgia's lawyers denied "the existence of any policy, practice or custom of limiting admission of the University of Georgia to white persons." Nor was this form of defense limited to higher education, where it sounded relatively plausible. Early in the case that brought about the integration of the Atlanta public schools, the defense claimed that the schools were not actually segregated; it was mere chance that resulted in there being all Negro teachers and students in some schools and all white teachers and students in others. This attitude can cause entertaining trials. At some point in every higher-education case, Mrs. Motley, who has handled practically all such cases for the Inc. Fund, always asks the university registrar what she calls "the old clincher": Would he favor the admission of a qualified Negro to the university? The registrar, often a strong segregationist himself, has to answer yes, as Danner did during the Georgia trial, and face the newspaper stories the next day that begin, as the Atlanta *Journal's* began, "The University . . . registrar has testified in Federal Court here that he favors admission of qualified Negroes to the University."

When I mentioned this to Mrs. Motley one evening in New York before I made my return trip to Georgia, she said, "It's not funny, really. The system is based on people getting on the stand and telling the truth. But people who talk about their respect for tradition and integrity and the Constitution get involved in one lie after another. They're willing to break down the system to keep a Negro out. In Mississippi, university officials got up on the stand and said they had never even discussed the Meredith case. They do the same kind of thing in voting cases. People are denied the right to vote not because they're Negroes but because they didn't dot an 'i' or interpret the Constitution correctly. This is one of the most serious by-products of segregation. The people get a disregard for the law. They see supposedly important people get up day after day on the stand and lie. The reason the whole thing seems funny to watch is that you spend all that time proving something everybody already knows."

To anybody who sat through the trial in the Athens Federal Building—to the reporters, who sat in the jury box, or to the university and town people, who segregated themselves by race the first day or two, even though they were in a federal court, and gradually got used to sitting wherever there was a place—it was no surprise to read Judge Bootle's decision that "although there is no written policy or rule excluding Negroes, including plaintiffs, from admission to the University on account of their race and color, there is a tacit policy to that effect" and that the plaintiffs "would already have been admitted had it not been for their race and color." However, Bootle's decision, issued one Friday afternoon in early January 1961, a month after the trial ended, did contain one surprise; it ordered the students admitted not by the following fall, as had been predicted, or for the spring quarter, beginning in March, but, if they so desired, for the winter quarter, for which registration closed the following Monday.

If the entire conspiracy against the state of Georgia had indeed stemmed from the intricate machinations of a foreign-looking man in New York, he could have picked no better place than the University of Georgia for the first confrontation, so it was ironic that this, the most cunning maneuver of all, was the result of two local accidents—the accident that the University of Georgia case got through the courts faster than the Atlanta school case, which had been filed two years earlier, and the accident that two seventeen-year-old high-school students happened to prefer the University of Georgia to Georgia State, probably because of the football team. There is no doubt that by 1961 the atmosphere in Georgia had benefited from the dismal example of other Southern states, and that the movement to keep the schools open, even with some desegregation, had spread from its normal base, consisting of housewives, to the ordinarily timid businessman. This was especially true after the Sibley Commission, a fact-finding committee created by the Georgia legislature, more or less as part of the Ritual, to gather opinion on segregation around the state, had submitted a surprising majority report urging that each community be given a choice of whether to close its schools or submit to desegregation. Still, most observers thought that if the first test came in Atlanta high schools in September 1961, as was expected, the result would be about the same as the result in New Orleans a year before. The Georgia legislature, dominated by representatives of the rural counties, might have enjoyed closing the Atlanta schools, or at least harassing them for the entertainment of the folks back home.

Closing the University of Georgia, where many of the legislators had gone to school, was a different matter. The university, ninety per cent Georgian, customarily had students from every county—no slight achievement in a state with 159 counties—and its graduates often went right back where they came from. The spell of the university was once explained to me by William Tate, its dean of men, who has been there for forty years and exchanges more affection with the university than any other man in the state. "When integration came, the university was the one institution that could weather it," Tate said. "There came a time when the people of the state of Georgia wanted the university not to close. A lot of people in the state love the university, and the university has always been tied up to the state. We usually have people here from every county—though sometimes we fudge a little to get one from Echols County or some little bitty place like that. We also have five hundred agricultural-extension workers and home-demonstration workers spread out all over the state. Our agriculture people have borne the brunt of shifting from a cotton economy to diversified farming. Ernest Vandiver, the last governor, was a graduate of the university. Carl Sanders, the present governor, is a graduate of the university. Both United States senators—Talmadge and Russell—are graduates of the university. Herman Talmadge's son is here and he is the fourth generation of Talmadges to attend the university. Richard Russell went here; his father was a trustee; his uncle was here. Why, he was the fourth Richard B. Russell here. I went down to speak in Greenville not long ago, and nine graduates came to hear me speak. Nine graduates right there in Meriwether County. It's not that way with Tech. The engineers don't drift back to these little old counties. There's not a soul in Meriwether

County who gives a damn what happens to Tech. When this thing happened I bet a lot of folks said, 'Hell, I get griped up a lot with that university. The students don't behave so well. I don't like the football. But it's a pretty good old university. It's helped us. They've done the best they can. They got their feet on the ground. And my granddaddy went there. I'll help them out.' "

If, by chance, there was a politician in Georgia at the time who thought Dean Tate's interpretation was overly sentimental, he could look at the record. The only political defeat of Eugene Talmadge, a Georgia graduate and one of the South's most adroit demagogues, came when he meddled with the university. That was in 1941, when the Board of Regents refused to fire a dean whom Governor Talmadge suspected of integrationist sympathies. Talmadge installed a new Board of Regents, which fired the dean, but a good number of angry teachers left as well, and the Southern Association of Colleges and Secondary Schools suspended the accreditation of the entire University System because of the political interference. In the next campaign, fought largely on the education issue, Talmadge could not shout about race loud enough to avoid an overwhelming defeat by Ellis Arnall, a liberal. Accreditation was restored, and a simple lesson was learned—that the voters of Georgia cared more for their university than their segregation.

Although, as it was later revealed, Governor Vandiver had advisers who thought he should make the gesture of going to jail before permitting the university to admit Charlayne and Hamilton (he had, after all, promised "not one, no, not one") there was never much doubt about what the governor would do or how the legislature, then gathering for its annual session in Atlanta, would react. On the day that Charlayne and Hamilton registered,

Vandiver finally announced that he would have to cut off
the university's funds, because the law required him to,
but that he would ask the legislature to change the law.
(The university planned to declare a five-day "holiday"
while this was being arranged.) He must have been
thankful that Judge Bootle enjoined him the next day
from using the law, at least providing Vandiver with the
opportunity to rail against the tyrannical federal judici-
ary for doing something he would otherwise have had to
do himself. Later, Vandiver offered the legislature his
alternative to all-out resistance: repeal of the segregation
laws, and the passage of a new group of laws, built around
a state tuition grant to parents who wanted to send their
children to private schools rather than to integrated public schools. According to the Ritual, Vandiver could not
call this retreat a retreat. He called it, instead, "the child-
protection freedom-of-association defense package." It
passed easily.

When I returned to Atlanta two and a half years later,
I was curious about the outcome of all the legislative and
judicial activity that had gone on during the integration.
I noticed in back issues of the Atlanta *Constitution* that
B. D. Murphy, Georgia's chief counsel at the Athens trial,
eventually presented a bill to the state for $14,500, plus
$248 in expenses. The total bill for outside counsel for the
Georgia trial, exclusive of the expenses of the Georgia
attorney general's office, was something over $25,000.

"The state got off cheap," an enlightened lawyer, wise
in the ways of Georgia politics, told me during my visit.
"It's just a matter of who loses gracefully, of course. But
this way the issue is settled. They got the best lawyer they
thought they could get, he lost, and nobody can say the
case was thrown or that the state should have had more

lawyers or that somebody else might have won. Why, we
fought election campaigns on that very issue after the decision outlawing the white primary. I don't begrudge them
the twenty-five thousand."

Governor Vandiver's "child-protection freedom-of-
association defense package" turned out to be an even
costlier form of the Ritual. The tuition-grant law—"the
basis of our defense," according to the governor—could
not mention segregation without being thrown out by the
courts; it therefore merely provided grants enabling any
child to attend an approved private school. But, as it
happened, not everybody in Georgia was willing to go
along with the game. A number of citizens took the law
at its word and claimed the grant it provided them, even
though they did not live in an integrated school district,
and even though, in most cases, their children were in
private schools anyway. The week I arrived in Atlanta,
the *Constitution* printed the names of 1200 Georgians
who had received tuition grants for the 1962-1963 school
year—the first year they were available. The *Constitution* pointed out that eighty-three per cent of the people
had had their children enrolled in private schools before
the law was passed. Among those listed were hundreds of
people outside Atlanta, which had the only integrated
schools in the state; a Negro educator in Atlanta, who was
sending his children North to prep school; and, one suspects, dozens of smiling integrationists. The *Constitution*
soberly printed letters from outraged citizens who pointed
out that the total cost of the tuition grants, $215,000, was
a lot of money to be handed out by a state that regularly
ranks among the last in the country on money spent for
public education. The legislature, equally alarmed,
changed the law so that a parent could apply for a tuition
grant only if the school board and the county authority of

his district had agreed that a "need" existed in the district. Even then, the request would have to go through the local board, and the grant had to be paid partially from local funds. "We expect this will cut this business down to nothing," a legislative assistant at the Capitol told me. That seemed to be the ideal arrangement for a law that was part of the Ritual; it would remain on the books for all to see but it could not be used enough to become expensive or embarrassing.

I also discovered, to my surprise, that Georgia still maintains a program of grants to Negro students who go outside the state to study subjects offered at one of the "white" institutions in the Georgia University System but not at one of the colleges it provides for Negroes. The out-of-state aid program was originated to give some semblance of "separate but equal" to a system that offered whites two large universities, a medical school, and a dozen other colleges across the state and offered Negroes three liberal-arts colleges that were once summed up easily by Tup Holmes as "a joke." Although Negroes can now legally attend any college in the system, the out-of-state aid program remains, perhaps to hold down the attendance of Negroes at colleges still considered white. (Charlayne could have received aid for studying journalism out of the state during her last two years in college.) The students annually receive the difference between the tuition they pay outside the state and what they would pay at a Georgia college, plus the equivalent of one round-trip railway coach ticket and a room-and-board supplement of $2.78 a week. The records for the 1961-1962 school year, which were the last available, showed that 1425 students were given out-of-state aid for study in thirty-four major fields at eighty-one institutions. Of these students, nine hundred and twenty-five were majoring in education. The total cost in 1961-1962 was $236,124.73, and the estimate for the next school year was about the same. In the 1962-1963 school year, then, Georgia, through tuition grants and out-of-state aid, was spending between $400,000 and $450,000 for the ritualistic protection of a custom that had already been violated. That was in addition to the cost of maintaining two separate school systems.

5

THE University of Georgia was desegregated with unusual suddenness. Only a week end separated Judge Bootle's surprise order and the appearance of Charlayne and Hamilton on the campus—not enough time for either the side of law or the side of violence to marshal its forces. A succession of contradictory court orders and ambiguous executive acts added to the confusion. At one point Judge Bootle stayed his own order, to allow time for an appeal, only to have Elbert Tuttle, chief judge of the Fifth Circuit, rescind the stay within a couple of hours. From the vague statements of Governor Vandiver and the refusal of President O. C. Aderhold to say anything at all, it was often not clear whether the university would remain open or not. The result of all the confusion was three relatively nonviolent, if chaotic, days for Charlayne and Hamilton, and a spate of congratulations to the university from tele-

50

vision newscasters and Northern newspapers on how well everybody had behaved.

Some of the undergraduates at Georgia had spent the week end rounding up signatures for petitions to keep the university open—the dominant concern of most students. Others had engaged in some minor effigy and cross burning, including a sorry demonstration I witnessed on the football practice field the Saturday night before Charlayne and Hamilton arrived. Twenty or so students wanted to burn a cross made of two-by-fours, but, owing to a lack of kerosene and a lack of experience in the art, they were unable to get it ablaze. Most of the demonstrations against integration during the new students' first three days on the campus seemed to be in that tradition. When Charlayne and Hamilton showed up at nine o'clock Monday morning, they were met only by a small group of curious students and a few reporters. In fact, throughout the first day, as Hamilton and his father and Horace Ward walked around campus going through the registration process, they often met with nothing more than some stares or a muttered "Hey, there's that nigger." The crowds around Charlayne were larger, but they seemed almost playful, even when they began to bounce a car she was riding in, or swarmed into the Academic Building, where she was registering, to yell, "Two-four-six-eight! We-don't-want-to-integrate!"—a chant they had borrowed from the women screaming at six-year-olds outside the integrated schools in New Orleans. A large crowd, triggered by a speech of Vandiver's that seemed to say the school would close, marched through downtown Athens on Monday night behind a Confederate flag. On Tuesday night, the first night Charlayne spent on campus, some of those who had found out which dormitory she had been assigned to—Center Myers—gathered on the street in front of it to chant, push around some television cameramen, and throw some fire-crackers. It was a rowdier crowd, but, like the rest, it was broken up single-handedly by Dean Tate, who confiscated some university identification cards and told some of the boys he knew to go home.

In a special issue of the campus newspaper Tuesday, ten student leaders issued a warning that violence could only mar the image of the university. By Wednesday just about everybody on the campus knew there was a riot scheduled in front of Charlayne's dormitory after the basketball game that night. It had been organized by a number of law-school students. All day Wednesday, the organizers scurried around making plans and bragging about the promises of help and immunity they had received from legislators. Some students got dates for the basketball game and the riot afterward. Reporters, faculty members, and even some students warned Joseph Williams, the dean of students, about the riot and suggested that he ban gatherings in front of the dormitory, or at least cancel the basketball game. But Williams said that neither step was necessary. Just after ten, a small crowd of students gathered on the lawn in front of Center Myers and unfurled a bed sheet bearing the legend "Nigger Go Home." Then three or four of them peeled off from the group, ran toward the dormitory, and flung bricks and Coke bottles through the window of Charlayne's room. Dean Tate had been assigned by Williams to remain with the crowd at the gymnasium after the basketball game, and Williams himself, standing in front of the crudely lettered sign, made no attempt to break up the group. As more people came up the hill from the basketball game— a close loss to Georgia Tech—and a few outsiders showed up, the mob grew to about a thousand people, many of them throwing bricks, rocks, and firecrackers. The few

Athens police present were busy directing traffic, and after about thirty minutes Williams finally acceded to the arguments of a reporter that the state police should be called. Although the university understood that thirty state troopers would be standing ready in their barracks outside Athens, the desk sergeant said that he could not send the troopers without the permission of the captain. But the captain said he had to have authority from the commissioner of public safety, and the commissioner, in turn, said he could not make a move without an order from the governor. In a failure of communications that still fascinates students of Georgia backroom shenanigans, it was so long before the governor gave the order that the state police did not arrive until an hour after the riot was over and, according to most estimates, two hours and twenty minutes after they were called. Then a carload of them came to take Charlayne and Hamilton back to Atlanta.

The riot was finally broken up by the arrival, together, of Dean Tate, who waded in and started grabbing identification cards, and of more Athens cops, who started fighting back when they were pushed and eventually drove everybody away with tear gas. It had been a nasty riot, but the group courage that sometimes comes to mobs had never infected it. Although the students could have stormed the dormitory several times without meeting any effective defense, they never did. A few hours after the television newscasters had congratulated Georgia on its behavior, the area around Center Myers looked like a deserted battlefield, with bricks and broken glass on the lawn, small brush fires in the woods below the dormitory, and the bite of tear gas still in the air. The casualties were several injured policemen, a girl on the second floor who had been scratched by a rock, and, as it turned out, the university's reputation. Dean Williams suspended

Charlayne and Hamilton, informing them that it was "for your own safety and the safety of almost seven thousand other students," and they were driven back to Atlanta. Williams' on-the-spot decision to suspend the target of the mob, rather than those in the mob itself, seemed unrelated to anybody's safety, since it was made after the last rioter had gone home and after university and Athens officials had assured him that order had been restored and that giving in to the mob would only mean going through the whole experience again. Dean Williams and Charlayne, who was crying by this time and clutching a statue of the Madonna, walked right out of the front door of Center Myers into the state police car, watched only by a few straggling reporters.

From the moment the two arrived on campus, Charlayne attracted much more attention than Hamilton. The reason was a great subject of debate among the reporters in Athens, some of whom devised complicated anthropological theories about greater interest in the enemy female. Others said it was only natural that unfriendly students should believe the girl more likely to be frightened away by their presence and that friendly students should think her more in need of their support. Dean Tate's answer is that it was merely a matter of convenience. He calculated that two or three times during the day there were two thousand students within two hundred yards of Charlayne, whose classes at the Henry W. Grady School of Journalism kept her on the busiest part of the campus, whereas there were far fewer students around the science center (which is removed from the main campus), where Hamilton spent most of the week. The fact that Charlayne took a dormitory room, while Hamilton moved in with a Negro family in Athens, made the difference even greater. Then, after the riot, stories about it, including a widely published picture of Charlayne leaving the dormitory in tears, made her better known to people outside Athens as well.

The immediate result of Charlayne's publicity was that in her first week or two at Georgia she received about a thousand letters—three or four times the number Hamilton got—from all over the United States and several foreign countries. Charlayne's mother filed all the letters by states, the Georgia and New York folders ending up the fattest, and later sent each of the writers a reprint of an article Charlayne wrote about her experience for a short-lived Negro magazine called the *Urbanite*. I was interested in seeing just what people wrote in such letters, and during my return visit to Georgia I borrowed the folders from Mrs. Hunter, who has them stored in a big pasteboard box. Charlayne told me later that the University of Georgia library would like to have the letters eventually but that she hesitated to give them up, especially while some of the writers might be embarrassed by even a historian's perusal of their names and opinions. That was an understandable objection, I thought, but it did seem like the justice of scholarship for the university to end up with one thousand expressions of outrage at its behavior. And they would make a good companion exhibit to the library's most famous historical document, the original Constitution of the Confederacy, a scroll that is said to be twelve feet long.

I was surprised to discover only fifteen or twenty abusive letters, and I was more surprised to find that most of the particularly foul ones were from the North. The unfriendly letters from the South, even if they were written in the guise of kindly advice, were instantly recognizable, since in almost every case they contained no conven-

tional salutation. "Dear Charlayne" would have been too
chummy, and anybody willing to say "Miss Hunter" apparently would not have written a letter in the first place.
Most of the writers solved the problem by starting out
with a flat "Charlayne Hunter," as if they were beginning
a formal proclamation.

There were also surprisingly few crank letters, although some of the writers were obviously just lonely
people who wanted somebody to write to, and a few of
the letters, like the one from Italy that began "Dear Little Swallow," reflected emotions other than sympathy. A
number were from Negro undergraduates (their own experiences with separate but equal education revealed in
their spelling) who sent along a picture and hoped that
a correspondence might develop. Many of the writers told
Charlayne they were praying for her; many of the Cath-
lics mentioned her conversion to Catholicism. She received dozens of prayer cards, copies of sermons by Harry
Emerson Fosdick and Norman Vincent Peale, Seventh
Day Adventist tracts, and two books by Gandhi. Several
letters were from college student councils or N.A.A.C.P.
chapters that had taken resolutions supporting Charlayne and deploring the action of those who persecuted
her. Most of the letters from individuals also expressed
admiration for Charlayne's "courage and dignity"—the
phrase was used almost as one word—and outrage at the
mob. There was often a mention of helplessness in the
letters from Northerners, which included phrases such as
"This must be small comfort" and "Of course, I can never
really understand." Some of those who believed they
could never really understand nevertheless tried to es-
tablish their credentials for understanding, listing personal experiences with prejudice or with Negroes. A girl
at the University of Connecticut told Charlayne that her

high school had a Negro teacher, who was considered by all the students to be the best teacher in the school; the yearbook had been dedicated to him four out of the five years he had been there. A young white woman in West Virginia said that she was attending a formerly all-Negro college. "YOUR people are teaching ME," she wrote. But the great majority of letters from the North had no personal experiences to offer. In many of them, a picture of Charlayne cut from a newspaper was enclosed, and most of them seemed to be from sensible, decent people who were appalled by the picture of a pretty girl being bullied by a mob and felt they had to write, even if they didn't know quite what to say.

The letters from Georgia had a different theme. Many of them were from University of Georgia alumni, who seemed to have a very specific and compelling reason for writing. They wanted to tell Charlayne that not all of them were like the mob or the people who permitted it to form. As I read through their letters, it seemed to me that each person who wrote felt he had to assure Charlayne of that or she might not know. On the whole, of course, the Georgia letters were also more realistic. But none quite captured the plain realism of a young boy in Rochester, New York, one of two dozen pupils in a parochial school eighth grade who had apparently written to Charlayne as a class project. "Dear Miss Hunter," he said. "I am very sorry for the way you are being treated. I hope you have the courage to take this treatment in the future. Respectfully yours."

I had first discussed the letters with Charlayne two years before, when she was back in Atlanta for the week end after her second week at the university. Since her return to the campus following the riot, she had been under police protection, and consequently she was now cut off from the rest of the students even more sharply than she had been during the chaotic first week. She seemed amazed and moved by the number of people who had written to her, but she found some of their letters slightly off the subject. "All these people say, 'Charlayne, we just want you to know you're not alone,'" she said, smiling. "But I look all around and I don't see anybody else."

Many reasonable people in Georgia, when they look back on what everybody calls "that night," believe that, all things considered, the riot was beneficial as well as inevitable—a nice clean shocker to polarize opinion, revolt decent citizens, and purge the violent of their anger. This line of thinking has never appealed much to Charlayne, who tends to be less dispassionate about the events of that night, but she admits that the reaction to the riot by the state and the university meant that she and Hamilton need no longer have any real fear about their physical safety. About the only public figure in the state who did not express outrage over the riot was Peter Zach Geer, who was then Governor Vandiver's executive secretary and later became lieutenant governor. He issued a statement, late that night, saying, in part, "The students at the University have demonstrated that Georgia youth are possessed with the character and courage not to submit to dictatorship and tyranny." Geer eventually found those ringing words a political liability. With almost everybody else in a mood for law and order, Governor Vandiver guaranteed that the peace would be maintained when, under a new court order, Charlayne and Hamilton returned to the campus the following Monday.

In their reaction to the riot, each of the groups involved in the situation—the state's politicians and the university's administration, faculty, and students—seemed to set the pattern for their future behavior. The university administration, looking around for somebody else to blame, eventually found the press (the group that had appeared most interested in preventing the riot) and "outsiders," represented by seven Knights of the Ku Klux Klan who had been arrested in their car on the campus that night. The Klansmen, sullen, ugly, and properly ominous, had been armed, and did afford an indication of what might have happened if the tear gas had not broken up the mob, but, as a matter of fact, they had left their arms in the car and had taken no real part in the riot. Nevertheless, they had guns and bad reputations, and were more logical suspects than respectable law students. Administration officials at first thought that a ban on student demonstrations would be undemocratic, but by the end of the week, finding the pressure for the ban greater than the pressure against it, they established a permanent policy of not putting up with overt hostility.

The faculty had maintained silence while the administration felt its way through the crisis, but with the riot and the suspension of Charlayne and Hamilton it almost exploded. A meeting was called the night after the riot, and eventually about four hundred faculty members signed a resolution that said, in part, "We insist that the two suspended students be returned to their classes." It was an extraordinarily strong statement for that time in Georgia; insisting that Negroes attend classes with whites was not a popular view, no matter what the circumstances. But the faculty went unpunished, and even when some professors organized groups to patrol the campus the first few nights Charlayne and Hamilton were back in Athens, there were no reprisals of any sort. The legislators in Atlanta noted the resolution with displeas-

ure but expressed their displeasure in no concrete action.
For their own part, they set up an investigating committee
called "The Special Committee Appointed on the 12th
Day of January, 1961, by the Speaker of the House of
Representatives of the General Assembly of the State of
Georgia to Find and Ascertain Facts Concerning the Certain Happenings and Episodes Surrounding the Admission of Two Negro Students to the University of Georgia." One of the facts the committee found and ascer-
tained was that "the majority of rocks were aimed at
Center Myers Dormitory and not at persons." Another
was that "many students feel they are being unduly re-
strained in exercising their right of freedom of assembly
and speech." But the legislators did not seem terribly interested, and sooner or later most of them actually appeared relieved to be done with the issue that had ab-
sorbed so much of their energy for so long.

The pattern of the students' attitude toward Charlayne and Hamilton emerged during the week of their
return. The fraternities and sororities let it be known
that anybody interested in his own position on campus
would be wise not to talk to the two Negroes. Another
group of students, most of them associated in one way or
another with Westminster House, the campus Presbyterian organization, formed a group called Students for
Constructive Action. They posted signs about the Golden
Rule in the classroom buildings and arranged to take
turns walking with Charlayne and Hamilton on their way
to classes. The girls in Center Myers had all trooped
down to visit Charlayne the first night she was in the
dormitory, reinforcing a widely held opinion that girls
would always be kind to a new girl, even a new Negro
girl. But on the following night, during the riot, their behavior changed drastically. After the first bricks had

crashed into her room, Charlayne went to a partly partitioned office, ordinarily used by one of the student counselors, and stayed there during most of what followed. A group of Center Myers coeds soon formed a circle in front of the office and marched around, each screaming an insult as she got to the door. "They had been told to strip their beds because tear-gas fumes might get into the sheets," Charlayne said to me later. "They kept yelling that they would give me twenty-five cents to make their beds, although at the hourly rate I was being paid by the N.A.A.C.P. according to them, it wouldn't have made much sense for me to work for a quarter. They kept yelling, 'Does she realize she's causing all this trouble?' Out of all the girls who had visited me the night before, only one girl came in and stayed in the office with me. But I finally made her go to bed. After a while, Mrs. Porter, the housemother, told me to get my things together because I was going back to Atlanta, and that's when I started to cry. Dean Williams carried my books and my suitcase, which was pretty nice. He could have made me carry them. When we went by to pick up Hamp, he wanted to drive his own car back. I guess by then my imagination was running wild; I could imagine KKK all up and down the highway. I didn't want Hamp to drive, and I almost got hysterical. Finally he said okay, he'd go with the troopers. Dean Tate went with us, and talked all the way back about the little towns we went through—things like why Dacula is pronounced Da*cu*la instead of *Dac*ula. The next day, at home, the lights were low, and people kept coming by saying how sorry they were. It felt as if I had been ill for a long time and was about to go, or as if somebody had already died. I was going back to Athens, but I was glad we didn't have to go back for two or three days."

6

Even before Charlayne had to return to Athens, a few days after the riot, another girl had decided to join her there as the university's first Negro graduate student. Mary Frances Early, a music teacher in the Atlanta public schools and a 1957 graduate of Clark, one of the colleges in the Atlanta University Center, had been studying for her Master's degree at the University of Michigan for three summers when she decided to transfer to the University of Georgia. She finished her work there in two summer sessions and a spring quarter, and became the first Negro to receive a degree from the university—almost a year before Charlayne and Hamilton graduated. Miss Early used Charlayne's room in Center Myers the first summer, and roomed there with Charlayne during the spring quarter and summer session of the following year. Before I left Atlanta for my return visit to Athens, I

62

stopped by Miss Early's house to ask her about her own experiences at Georgia and how she thought Charlayne had managed. A direct young lady, and formerly the music columnist for the militant Atlanta *Inquirer*, Miss Early admitted frankly that she had enrolled at Georgia for the Cause.

"I sent for an application two days after the riot," she told me. "I thought that since the undergraduate school was open, somebody should go to the graduate school, and when I saw a picture of Charlayne that night, holding that Madonna, I knew I had to go. I had a little trouble about transferring. Mr. Danner told me that the University of Georgia was under no obligation to accept credits from Michigan and that it would be silly for me to lose all that time. I told him the time would not be lost anyway and that I wanted to go to Georgia. I think after Charlayne and Hamilton went in we thought in Atlanta that once it was open everything would be okay. But that was far from the case. When I saw that room, I was shocked. It was completely isolated from everybody else."

Most of the ground floor of Center Myers is taken up by a vast, ugly lobby, but there are identical apartments at opposite ends of the floor. One of them is occupied by the housemother; the other was apparently intended for a counselor. It has a bedroom, a living room, a kitchenette, and a private bathroom, and it seemed to the university officials a good place to put Charlayne when, in spite of their offer to waive a rule requiring all girls under twenty-three to live on campus, she decided to live in a dormitory. The Women's Student Government Association leaders who had been living in the apartment were asked to move out, and they made no complaints about leaving its lonely splendor to return to their sorority houses. When Charlayne returned after the riot, she found that the university, sensitive about the way editorialists and legislators had been tossing around the word "suite," had shut off the bedroom. It was reopened the following spring, when Miss Early joined Charlayne in the suite, and it was kept open when two Negro freshmen moved in with her in the fall of her senior year.

"That first summer, I didn't realize how lonely it was until one time when I wanted somebody to zip up my dress in the back, and there was nobody in a nearby room I could ask," Miss Early told me. "When I went back for the spring quarter, both Charlayne and I wanted single rooms that were private but not isolated. There are only freshmen in Center Myers during the regular term, and I requested a room in a dorm where there would be somebody near my own age. But they said there were no other rooms available. Of course, the first week of that quarter, Charlayne and I had lunch with a graduate student, an older woman, who said she was changing dorms because of the vacancies in a new dorm that had opened. I kept wondering, Just how naïve do they think we are? Their excuses are so thin a child could see through them. I know Charlayne was upset that she couldn't get a room in another dorm, especially this year. A senior housed with freshmen, that's not right."

Even if she and Charlayne had had a lot in common with the younger girls, Miss Early went on, the atmosphere in the dormitory would have been cool. "If you went to the lobby to watch TV, there was usually no discourse, although occasionally a word or two was said," she told me. "It just wasn't the kind of atmosphere it should have been after almost two years. We never went into anybody else's room, since we were never invited. I didn't know until last summer how the upstairs looked. We had nine Negroes in the summer school then, so they had to put some in connecting suites upstairs. During the spring quarter, there were three girls who used to come down to the room. We had dinner with them one evening, and they explained that they wanted to be more friendly but that they were rushing sororities and had been told by some of their big sisters that they were treading on dangerous ground. After that, they came much less often, though they did continue to come."

Before arriving at Georgia for her first summer, Miss Early said, she received a letter from James Popovich, a speech professor who had also tried to be helpful to Charlayne and Hamilton. Except for occasional meetings with Popovich and one or two other faculty members, Miss Early was alone. "It was very lonely that first summer," she told me. "Since Hamp and Charlayne were gone, I was the only one there, and I was almost ostracized. I normally ate at the Student Center cafeteria, and that first summer I ate lunch with others only twice. Often, when I entered, the students would start these wailing noises—something like a cat. But nobody ever said anything. Oh, once a student turned back to me in the line and asked if I was a student. Of course I answered in the affirmative. I'm not what they call a trouble-maker, and I never sat down at a table with other persons except if it was crowded and I had to, and then, most of the time, they would get up. Once, one boy stayed, but he finished very quickly. It's not that they were all prejudiced; they thought they'd suffer socially. There was only one incident. One day, somebody threw a lemon and hit me in the back. I was very angry that anybody would be so immature, and I didn't go back for several days. But Doctor Popovich said that was just what they wanted, so then I went back. Corky King, the Presbyterian minister, and his wife and one of their children ate with me the first day.

"I went to the Co-op, the snack bar, just once—one day

when the whole vocal class went for coffee. Everybody just plunked down a dime at the register, and I did the same thing, but as I walked away the boy at the register yelled, 'Hey, you, come here!' He was a very coarse-talking boy. I didn't turn around and he yelled again. Everybody was staring, so I went back and said, 'Are you talking to me?' And he said, 'Yeah, are you a student here?' I told him I was, and he said, 'Show me your I.D. card.' I did, and went on. But it put a damper on everything. I never went back there. When you ask where we could go—well, some of the places perhaps we could go but you don't know how you'll be received, so you don't go for fear of being embarrassed. Everybody wants to be comfortable. But sometimes, when it's necessary, you have to go anyway."

By joining the university chorus her first summer, Miss Early became the first Negro to participate in any extracurricular activity at Georgia. That summer, she said, she was "tolerated, but that's all" by the other members. In fact, she became the only girl in the chorus who had to have her own individual sheet music, because the girl she was supposed to look on with felt that handling the same music was more contact than she cared to have. "By the second summer," Miss Early said, "there were three of us in the chorus, and that made things easier. They seemed to get used to us and forget our color, and after a while it was fine. More students just have to be seen in more places. After a while, it becomes natural."

As a member of the chorus, Miss Early ran into a problem that Charlayne had found particularly irritating the first year she was at Georgia. Two or three months after she and Hamilton entered the university, Donald Hollowell and the lawyers from the state asked Judge Bootle to rule on just how thoroughly integrated Georgia was, according to his original order. To no one's surprise, Bootle ruled that Charlayne and Hamilton and the Negro students who followed them were entitled to attend all university events without being segregated and to use all the facilities of the university. Soon after the ruling was handed down, I saw Charlayne in Atlanta, and she seemed angrier at the university administration than she had ever been before. She had planned to return to Athens that Saturday night for a play, taking along a date from Atlanta. The adviser in the dean's office assigned to her, after learning that the date was a Negro, checked with her superiors and informed Charlayne that the university was completely integrated as far as she and Hamilton were concerned but that the order did not include other Negroes. By the following summer, when Miss Early wanted to bring her mother and some friends to a concert of the chorus, the university had found a less direct and more characteristic way of handling the problem. She was told to check with Dean Williams before bringing other Negroes on the campus, but she was unable to get an appointment with him until after the concert was over. When she finally did see him, he said it wouldn't have been a very good idea anyway, because the university was not ready for such a step.

When I remarked on Charlayne's anger at the incident of the play, Miss Early said, "I think Charlayne often feels that it's a sign of weakness to complain, and tries to pretend everything is okay. But she knows it isn't, and sometimes it comes out. I think the whole thing has affected her more than she cares to admit. She's been sick a lot, and it's no wonder. I knew her before, and she used to be so carefree and gay. Now she's only carefree and gay on the outside."

Although Charlayne did not seem quite carefree and
gay the first time I saw her in Athens that week, she did
seem remarkably like a normal coed. She was even wearing a University of Georgia pin on her sweater when I
found her in the Journalism Building, chatting with Joan
Zitzelman, a graduate student of journalism who was
probably her closest friend at Georgia, and two or three
other journalism students. Charlayne suggested that I
have lunch with her at the Continuing Education Center,
and we drove up the long hill from Main Campus to a
huge, modern red-brick building across the street from
Center Myers. The Continuing Education Center—or
C.E., as it is usually called—serves as a hotel and convention center not only for university conferences but for
dozens of nonacademic meetings as well. It has a restaurant, and that is where Charlayne usually ate during
her last two years at Georgia, since she believed that the
food in the student dining hall she had used during her
first spring there had disagreed with her and may have
contributed to the attacks of stomach trouble she suf-
fered, off and on, during her stay. The C.E. restaurant
caters mostly to faculty members and conference delegates, and the latter were frequently amazed to find
Charlayne, in person, right in the same restaurant. "We
get a lot of people like the county clerks meeting there,"
a liberal professor later told me cheerfully. "They're all
dyed-in-the-wool conservative Baptists. They've come to
accept the fact that Charlayne and Hamilton are in
school here, but seeing her eat there with a couple of
white boys really shocks them." Charlayne was also a
good customer of the C.E. coffee shop, and as we passed
it, on the way to the restaurant, she called out a friendly
hello to one of the waitresses and to the woman who op-
erated the magazine stand.

I told Charlayne that the atmosphere at the Journalism Building had seemed surprisingly easy. "Oh, I feel pretty comfortable in the Journalism School now," she replied. "I'm never left alone in the corner without anybody to talk to, and now I don't feel any reluctance about walking up to a group of people. I know most of the students and professors."

Charlayne's general good will toward the Journalism School did not extend to the student newspaper, the *Red and Black*, or to its editor, Larry Jones, who had written a column that day on Hamilton Holmes. The column was based on a news report of Hamilton's speech before the Savannah Council on Human Relations. Hamilton had said that he had made no friends at the university, and although the observation had been made in answer to a question, the news story made it appear to be the main line of a speech devoted principally to complaint. Jones had objected strenuously. "Holmes entered the University forcibly, as an alien," Jones wrote. "He attended as an alien. And when he graduates this June (with honors, I understand) he will still be an alien. The treatment he has received; the friendless atmosphere he has encountered: he could have expected no more and he has received no less. . . . On this 'friendless' campus with its 'less than cordial' atmosphere, Mr. Holmes has gone his own way. He has devoted much time to scholastic endeavors and little to anything else. (By this I mean extra-curricular activities.) He had no choice. He made his choice when he entered Georgia two years ago. So perhaps my resentment of his complaints is wrong. After all, there's not much for him to do but study and make speeches."

Charlayne said that Hamilton was badly upset by the column. "It's hard to reassure him," she said. "He doesn't have much contact with the students. It wouldn't have

bothered me as much, knowing what halfwits some of
those people are. Can you imagine! All Hamp is is an
honor student. Isn't that terrible! And the article wasn't
even checked to find out if it was accurate. They're supposed to be journalists! I was thinking all during history
class of what I'd write Jones. I couldn't even take any
notes. But I decided I wouldn't get down to that level, and
on any other level they wouldn't understand it."

Strolling around the Georgia campus, as I did that
same afternoon, I found it easy to understand how Hamilton might have reached his most dejected point exactly a
year before. In the spring, the University of Georgia is no
place for an alien. Georgia looks very much like the campus of that college that Hollywood movies used to call
"State." One professor told me that on the day he arrived
there from the Midwest he had expected to see "Jeanne
Crain racing across the quad, her hair blowing in the
wind." Almost every building is some combination or
other of red brick and white columns, from the solid-
looking pillared brick library to the ornate white-
columned ante-bellum fraternity and sorority houses on
Milledge Avenue, some of them carefully marked not only
with Greek letters but also with numbers assigned them
by the Athens Historical Society when it devised its tour
of the city. It was a warm day, with the dogwood out and
the big oaks on the quadrangle of Main Campus starting
to turn green. At the Chi Phi house, a block from the
Journalism Building, the brothers, most of them in Ber-
muda shorts and T-shirts, were making good use of their
vast front lawn, practicing for the softball season, flying
kites, and frolicking with their new mascot, a goat. Next
door, at Kappa Alpha, the most noisily Southern of all the
fraternities, more softball was being played, under a huge

Confederate flag that had been lowered to half mast during the first three days Charlayne and Hamilton were on
the campus, had been raised again when they were suspended, and then, after a word from the Dean's office,
had stayed where it was upon their return. I had seen the
Kappa Alphas raise the flag in a wild midnight celebration
of the mob's victory in driving Charlayne from the campus—a scene that seemed far removed from springtime
softball.

Main Campus, the original site of the university, is a
huge double quadrangle that starts at the edge of downtown Athens and extends southward for half a mile. It is
entered through an arch that is often pictured in the university's literature. On the lawn nearby is a large sign saying, "The University of Georgia. Founded in 1785." The
sign is accurate only in a broad and rather unscholarly
way. The university was chartered in 1785, but it did not
have such basic equipment as students or a campus until
sixteen years later. The University of North Carolina, for
one, was a going operation by that time, and, in fact, had
been provided for in the state constitution before 1785.
Only Georgia, however, had a specific charter for a university at that date, and it often refers to itself, with a
careful use of the superlative, as "The Oldest Chartered
State University in the Country." The University of Georgia did not award its first doctorate until the time of the
Second World War—the University library's list of Master's theses and doctoral dissertations written between
1868 and 1950 includes only six for doctorates, five of
them in education—so, like many a Southern university
that was not the oldest chartered state university in the
country, it relied for years on graduates of Virginia and
North Carolina to make up its faculty. Still, in many ways,
Georgia can claim a long tradition. The all-important

charter was drawn up by Abraham Baldwin, a Yale man
from Connecticut, who modeled it on Yale's. Baldwin
became a United States Senator from Georgia and also
served as first president of the university for sixteen years
—a term that was not disturbed by the presence of students or the acquisition of buildings but did resolve the
haggling over a site for the university. In 1801, when Jo-
siah Meigs, another Yale man, took over, Athens had
been chosen, and Meigs started to build Old College,
whose design was almost identical with that of Connecticut Hall, one of Yale's earliest buildings. Old College is
still standing. Planted in the middle of the lawn, it forms
the common line for the two quadrangles of Main Campus. Except for the absence of window shutters and the
presence of two or three lovely dogwood trees nearby,
it might be taken for Connecticut Hall. Since Old College
went up, Georgia's relations with Mother Yale have been
fitful. An attempt in the middle of the nineteenth century to bring the New England elm to Main Campus was
an almost total failure. An annual Georgia-Yale football
game, started in the twenties, lasted for a dozen years,
and the dedication of the Georgia football stadium was
marked by a Yale game in Athens, but Georgia football
historians say it is mere coincidence that Yale and Georgia have the only two major college football teams called
the Bulldogs. Many of the buildings on Main Campus do
have a blocky, New England look, and a dozen of them
are more than a century old. The Demosthenian Literary
Society, which occupies one of the oldest buildings in the
quadrangle, was founded in 1803—a long time ago, even
by Yale standards—and Demosthenian's rival, Phi Kappa,
which faces it across the quad, was founded only a few
years later.

One traditional campus decoration that I had missed

at Georgia during my first visit there was the assemblage of posters covering bulletin boards and store windows usually found around most college campuses. Advertisements for lectures, concerts, or plays were nowhere in sight. On my first day back, I walked over to see what the main bulletin board, next to the university chapel, had to offer, and found it almost empty. There were some advertisements for textbooks, car parts, a parachute, and various appliances; some rental offers for cabins on a lake near the campus; some requests for rides to Brunswick or Savannah; and a permanent announcement that "Demosthenian Literary Society invites all Male Students to their Wednesday night meeting," an indication that Demosthenian was not literary in a finicky way. The biggest signs on the board were for a Spring Fever Dance (sponsored by the Student Center) and a Kappa Alpha Theta Kite Flying Contest.

"Actually, a large number of things go on," Frank Gibson, a political-science professor, told me later, "but you'd never know it from walking around the campus. We have a good concert series; the philosophy department has brought in some outstanding speakers. Perhaps because all these events are attended almost exclusively by faculty members, they don't bother to advertise. The faculty already knows about them."

Gibson said the university has lately made good progress in improving its faculty and facilities (according to the latest Report of the President, Georgia managed to increase the percentage of Ph.D.s on its faculty from 27.7 in 1952 to 47.1 in 1962, even though, the Report noted, "faculty salaries are still too low to permit competition with above average institutions") but that "the student interest is still in non-academic things. Demosthenian and Phi Kappa hold debates on Wednesdays, and all you have to do to become a member is attend a couple of debates. But they don't draw much of a crowd and they have no real influence. As the campus is organized now, most of the grouping is strictly social in nature."

This grouping, Gibson told me, had a good deal to do with how Charlayne and Hamilton were treated. "Being friendly to them is still not totally acceptable among social fraternities, and the whole social life of the university rests in fraternities and sororities," he said. "The university is simply not equipped to handle the independent student. The Student Center is very poor—a run-down old building with a pool room and a ballroom—and the town offers limited facilities. I have a girl in one of my classes who's a transfer student and is not in a sorority. She's a psychology major, and most of her friends are in the Psychology Department, just as many of Charlayne's friends are in the Journalism School. I think there has been some progress toward acceptance of the Negroes on campus. It's partly a matter of personality. Hamilton—in outward appearance, at least—is semi-surly. His look more or less says, 'Don't approach me.' I notice that the Negro freshman boy who came this year is always with a group, while Hamilton is always alone. I see the Negro freshman girls coming and going on their way to classes, and they are almost always alone. On the other hand, I've never seen Charlayne alone. I think in some ways there's less of a barrier now between her and the rest of the students than there was at the beginning."

As I walked around the campus with Charlayne that week, there often appeared to be no barrier at all, and her life at Georgia seemed unrelated to the stories I had heard from Mary Frances Early. Sometimes she gave the impression of being just another college girl—studying in the library with other students, or asking a boy if she could borrow his notes for a history class she had missed, or chatting with a professor about the parking problem (quite a problem in a university with nine thousand students who maintain forty-two hundred cars), or answering another girl's questions about a surprise quiz in philosophy, or standing with the other members of her honors seminar in the art, music, and drama of the twentieth century and nodding in sympathy as one of the girls said, "Y'all, that last play, *The Seagull*—I just could not fathom that." But often I would look around to see students staring, and three times during the week a group of boys passing in a car shouted insults. Charlayne took no notice of either the stares or the shouts.

One morning, when Charlayne had a free hour between social-and-intellectual history and introduction to philosophy, an hour she had promised herself to devote to reading *The Seagull* and other unfathomables, we went for coffee to the Co-op, the snack bar near the Journalism School. On the walk over from the history building, two or three students and an instructor called out greetings, and one boy stopped Charlayne to say hello and ask how her classes were going. The Co-op, a cramped, low-ceilinged room done in knotty pine, looked like the product of the same set designer who had done Main Campus, the arch, the Varsity (a hamburger hangout across the street from the arch), and most of the other buildings at Georgia.

I had asked Charlayne if many unpleasant remarks were made to her as she walked around the campus, and as we entered the Co-op she said, "Well, if you're going to hear any remarks, you'll probably hear them here. Whenever there's a big crowd, you can expect to hear something as I walk past the tables along the front wall." As it happened, we got nothing but stares as we walked in and took a knotty-pine booth near the serving line. When I asked Charlayne why she came to the Co-op if it seemed likely that somebody would say something insulting, she said, "Well, it doesn't happen *every* day. And it's not that bad. It's not the whole group, and I don't sit with those boys. And sometimes I get hungry in the morning. Anyway, I usually come in earlier—sometimes with Joan or somebody from the Journalism School, and sometimes alone. When I'm alone, sometimes people sit down with me and sometimes they don't. Sometimes they talk and sometimes they don't. I usually don't want to talk to anybody in the morning anyway. It's hard to say how often I hear somebody make a remark. I guess I could calculate a way to avoid it for, say, a week. But I would have to stay away from certain areas—here, in front of the Kappa Alpha house, that tree that the law students gather around in front of the Journalism Building. But it's not so bad now. The K.A.s usually don't yell nasty things now; they just yell my name. I might even go a couple of weeks sometimes. Last summer, I went for a long time without anybody saying anything. At the Continuing Education Center, people stare a lot, but they never say anything. Oh, one time a man kept saying, 'There's that little nigger who caused all the trouble.' He kept saying it quite loud and some women with him were trying to stop him. I usually don't pay any attention, but that time I got mad. I just stared back at him all through dinner. Or for a while. Then I just said, 'What the heck.'

"We'd always feel little tremors here during things like the Freedom Ride and Ole Miss. Then the catcalls would start again, but not bad. The first half year, they used to let the air out of my tires a lot, but after that nothing really out of the ordinary happened." Pointing out a boy

standing near the cash register, Charlayne said, "There's
the guy who asked Mary Frances for her I.D. card. He
made me show mine once, too. Maybe he asked Mary
Frances because he really didn't know she was a student."
She paused, then added, "No, I guess he's kind of mean."

A few minutes later, another journalism student and
an instructor from the Journalism School joined us,
and then a husky student with a heavy Georgia accent
leaned over the booth and said, "hey, Charlayne, you have
any extra pillows?"

"Why?" Charlayne asked.

"We're going to tar and feather Doctor Kopp," the boy
said, referring to a journalism professor. "I thought that
chocolate-covered ground glass I gave him for Christmas
would end that kind of Public Opinion exam."

Soon after that, another student approached the table,
looked over the top of the booth quickly, then, smirking
and without having said a word, went back to a table
near the front wall where he had been sitting with a
group of boys.

"That's one of the guys on the paper," Charlayne said.
"He's the one who was running for some office and
sent around a form letter for support, and the salutation
on mine said 'Dear Nig.' He probably wants to see who's
with me." She smiled. "He likes to keep up with my progress and activities."

Charlayne's own tenure on the *Red and Black* was
short and unpleasant. She had had an unusual amount of
experience for a journalism student, having written for
the *Inquirer* throughout her stay at Georgia and worked
for the Louisville *Times* in the summer of 1961, but her
Journalism School faculty adviser suggested that she work
at least one quarter on the student newspaper, a bi-
weekly of high-school quality, put out mainly by journal-

ism students. In the fall quarter of her senior year she
worked in the advertising section, making up dummies
for ads and devising an advertising filing system. "I
didn't want to barge into the editorial end," she told me.
"I would have had to go out and talk to a lot of people I
didn't want to talk to. I worked mainly with Tommy Johnson, the business manager, who's a pretty nice guy. We
usually worked Tuesday nights, making up the ad dummy
for the editorial people to fill the next night. But one
Wednesday night, when we went to the weekly criticism,
the editor asked everybody to stay, because they were
short of people. Tommy had left for some reason. I stayed,
but I just sat there. They went around asking everybody
if he could print. Nobody could, so I finally said I could
print, just because I wanted something to do. I got
through with the printing, and the editor kept asking people to do things, but he would never ask me. So finally I
just left. I never went back."

7

THE man at the University of Georgia who most often
ends up dealing with problems of student behavior—and
the only university official who seemed significantly interested in keeping order during the first week Charlayne
and Hamilton were on the campus—is William Tate, who
has been dean of men for seventeen years and, except
for a few years as a prep-school English teacher, has been
at the university since 1920, when he arrived as a freshman from Pickens County, in north Georgia. Early in my
second visit to Athens, I went to talk to Tate about how
the students had acted during the first week of integration and how they had acted since. His philosophy during
that first week was merely "to keep some of the boys who
feel strongly from making fools of themselves," but both
Charlayne and Hamilton came to believe soon after their
arrival that the dean's extraordinary concern for his students and his university included a concern for them.

Tate's methods of keeping order vary greatly with the situation. One morning, during the first few days of integration, while Hamilton was being taken on an orientation tour of the library, I saw Dean Tate approach a crowd of boys who had gathered in front of the building. He looked them over for a moment, then began to talk to them about what the library was made of. The columns, he said, were of Indiana limestone and the steps of Georgia granite. The lobby, though, was made of Georgia marble, from around Tate, Georgia, where his family had run the marble works for many years, and, the dean assured his audience, some day, after years and years of wear, there would be nothing standing of the library but the lobby. The boys laughed and drifted away. When a crowd was more threatening, the back-home stories of the Dean's life in the Salacoa Valley were replaced by the confiscation of a student's identification card in an astonishing operation that combined an iron grip to prevent the prisoner from escaping, a swift movement toward the wallet to help the boy find the card, and a kindly hold to keep the terrified boy from falling. Dean Tate is a big man, with most of the fifty or sixty pounds he has gained since his career as a Georgia cross-country runner settled in jowls and stomach, but he is still too agile to be eluded by many undergraduates. A prominent nose, a tiny mouth, eyes squinting out of gold-rimmed glasses, and hair cut short on the sides like an Army sergeant's give Tate the look of a gigantic, thoughtful owl—especially if he happens to be leaning back in his chair trying to recall the name of an ancestor or the position of a Georgia football player.

"First I always say, 'Gimme your I.D. card,'" he said, when I asked him about his preferred method of handling a crowd. "I don't talk with them or tell them anything. Their first instinct is to give it to me, and, more often than not, they do. I help them with it sometimes. You notice that out there I didn't let them get around me, or get me over here and them over there. I move among them. I get personal. I call the names of the ones I know. I say, 'Henry, what you doing over here?' That's a big psychological thing—a technique, you might call it." In Tate's view, however, his success in dealing with the crowds during desegregation lay in more effective weapon than technique: his background.

"One thing that was never forgotten in all of that hullaballoo is that I wasn't a Yankee," he said. "That big segregationist who was out there offering to put up bond for anyone arrested called me Bill all evening. After all, I was here. My brothers were here. I married a girl whose grandfather was chancellor. I have four grandparents and six great-grandparents buried in Georgia. You can't have but eight great-grandparents, you know. There was no question I wasn't a Yankee. There was the knowledge that this guy who's taken up for the nigger, he's sort of one of us. Things might have been different if it had been a man from the University of Pennsylvania or Harvard. I'm essentially provincial, you know. I used to say I consider South Carolina the Deep North, Alabama the Far West, and Florida the tropics." Of the University of Georgia alumni who sent Dean Tate letters concerning his role as the protector of the Negroes, ninety per cent praised his actions.

"I think the main thing that has changed among the students since that first week is that we no longer have the boys who felt they could keep them out," Tate continued. "That group has disappeared—either graduated or flunked out." The leaders of that group, I recalled, had been law students, who seemed to be interested in practical politics rather than political theory, and who apparently thought that resisting desegregation was the way to the legislature. (Their favorite forum was the Demosthenian Literary Society, whose dominant concern for several years had been ultra-conservative political causes.)

"Well, old Dean [J. Alton] Hosch over at the law school is very sensitive about that," Dean Tate said. "I'll tell you, in every state law school you have in the lower section of your class some of the great future leaders of the state. Whenever you have a law school in the state, some people who think they're going to be governor are going to be there—in the lower section. Naturally, the Supreme Court decision is something a law school ought to be interested in, and these people are. There were just three Law School boys leading that group, and all of them flunked out. Well, two of them flunked out and the other didn't pass the bar exam down here at Milledgeville, and he's an insurance adjuster or something. I think we're getting along pretty well now. Oh, we had to call in one or two boys. A boy in the cafeteria used to throw down the change on Charlayne's plate; sometimes a nickel would land in the squash or a dollar in the iced tea. I called him in here and I said, 'I'm just going to tell you one thing and I'm not going to say any more and then I want you to come back and talk to me in a day or two.' I told him, 'I'm hired by the university and when you work in the line in the cafeteria so are you. I don't care how you feel about things. You're being paid by an institution whose policies are otherwise.' A day or two later he came in and said he decided I was right."

The current attitude of most students toward the whole affair, Dean Tate thought, amounted to a sheer lack of interest. It did seem logical that students in the mainstream of Georgia social life should have no more interest in Negro undergraduates than they had in anybody else who was not a member of their own group—especially if any show of unfavorable interest was likely to get them involved with Dean Tate. "Both Charlayne and Hamilton have gotten along okay," Tate said. "I think the students have been friendlier to Charlayne. Hamilton's got a very intelligent view of the whole thing, but he's not exactly an extrovert."

In the two and a half years since Hamilton and Charlayne returned to a chilly peace on the campus after the riot, the routine of Hamilton's life at Georgia had not changed—or, as Hamilton, always literal and exact, put it the first time I saw him on my second visit to Athens, "I haven't been able to detect any difference if there is any." Hamilton still roomed with an Athens family named Killian and took all his meals at Killian's Four Seasons, a small restaurant that the family operates next to their gray frame house. As Hamilton began his final ten-week quarter at Georgia, he had never eaten in a university dining hall, studied in the library, used the gymnasium, or entered the snack bar. He had no white friends outside the classroom. No white student had ever visited him, and he had never visited one of them. He had, as his father told me, "lived for Friday," and had driven the seventy miles to Atlanta every week end since his enrollment. He could sum up his social life at the university in a few sentences: "I've gone to almost all the plays—three or four a year. I usually go alone on Thursday night. I've been to the football games. I haven't gone to any basketball games because they're on Saturday night. There's better basketball in Atlanta—plus I'd have to stay here all day Saturday, and I can't be fighting that."

Hamilton's approach to the situation he found himself

in at Georgia could be defined as simple combat—combat
that he had already won to the extent of being elected to
Phi Kappa Phi, a scholastic honorary society. "One thing
stuck in the back of my mind the whole time," he said.
"Danner got up on the stand in that trial and said if they
had to take somebody, okay, they might take Char some
day but I wasn't qualified. That made me mad. But look,
that guy said I wasn't qualified and here I end up with
one of the highest averages in the school. You know,
when I went to Morehouse I just fell in love with the
place; I had made a frat and I was playing football and I
didn't want to push it. But shoot, I figured we had gotten
into this thing and we couldn't back out. Then, after that
interview and the way they brought it up in court, I was
raring to come down here and show them. That's why I got
such a kick out of Danner coming up after my election
to Phi Kappa Phi and congratulating me. He's in Phi
Kappa Phi too. It used to be he wouldn't talk to me on
the campus. Now he almost crosses the street to see me."

Nobody else crossed the street to see Hamilton; practically nobody else even acknowledged his existence.
There were some stares, and occasionally, while he was
walking across the campus, he heard a remark flung from
a passing car. However, unlike Charlayne, Hamilton,
husky, athletic-looking and usually wearing a scowl, had
never been jeered at by a student passing him on foot.
"There's one little boy that every time he sees me in his
car he has something to say, but when I pass by him on
the campus he doesn't say a word," Hamilton told me.
"I guess they're never quite sure of what I might do. With
the girls they don't have to worry." Although Hamilton's
address and phone number were listed in the student
directory, the Killians had experienced no harassment
after the first week or so. "I haven't had any trouble, ex-

cept a few months ago I had somebody to flatten all the tires on my car, and they tore the chrome off my car once," Hamilton said. "But that's about all, except the incident at the frat house." The incident at the frat house, as Hamilton had revealed in a television interview a year after it happened, occurred when he parked his car near the Kappa Alpha house and went into the infirmary down the street to visit Charlayne. He came out to find his car blocked by another car and a crowd of boys in a belligerent mood waiting to see what he would do about it. Hamilton eventually reached into his car for a flashlight and, holding it in his pocket and pretending it was a gun, persuaded the boys to move their car. After the incident at the frat house, Hamilton was bothered even less.

One cause of Hamilton's isolation was, of course, mere physical distance. Killian's, to which I drove one night during my stay in Athens to have dinner with him, is a mile from the campus, and Hamilton invariably covered the distance alone in a car. Moreover, his courses did not give him any reasonably small base of operations, where people could get to know him. "I haven't actually cultivated any close friendships," Hamilton explained. "Char sees those people in journalism all the time. In pre-med, about the time I get to know somebody, we're separated and I don't see him again." But another cause of Hamilton's isolation, as Dean Tate had told me, was his own personality. Unlike Charlayne, or most of the rest of his own family, Hamilton does not have an easy flow of words. He answers questions directly but is not troubled by silence —an attitude that may stem from a serious childhood speech impediment, which has left only an occasional, almost imperceptible block in his speech. Hamilton's manner in the Athens Negro community, where he was well known and well liked, was about that of any amiable, suc-

cessful athlete—a quick, friendly nod to one of the "street
boys," a tap on somebody's shoulder as he walked into
Killian's. I remembered a lunch at Killian's during the
tense second week of integration when Hamilton, who had
to face the crowd once more for an afternoon class, was
pacing up and down the restaurant, obviously, if silently,
nervous. Charlayne, who was through with classes for the
day, had looked up in mock concern and said, "Hamp,
would you like for me to walk you to class?"

When I arrived at the Killian house, Hamilton was
changing out of his basketball clothes for dinner. He
played basketball at the Negro Y.M.C.A. almost every afternoon, he told me—partly to keep his eye in shape for
the basketball he played on Saturdays in Atlanta and
partly just for something to do. His schedule had changed
only insofar as the times of his classes and labs had
changed from quarter to quarter—classes in the morning,
back to Killian's for lunch, classes and basketball in
the afternoon, Killian's for dinner, studying. His Atlanta
schedule had also remained the same. "With me nothing
had changed," Hamilton said. "When I go to Atlanta, I
play basketball with the same boys I played with before. I
have the same girl friend. I still work as a lifeguard in
the summer. It's all the same." Before we left for dinner,
Hamilton got a phone call from Alice Henderson and
Kerry Rushin, the two Negro freshmen from Atlanta who
were then sharing Charlayne's suite in Center Myers.
They asked him to pick them up so they could eat dinner at Killian's and study there, and Hamilton agreed
right away. As we drove in to get them, he explained to
me that he and Charlayne and Mattie Jo Arnold, a graduate student in music who roomed off campus, did a lot of
chauffering for the girls, who had no car and would
otherwise have been isolated. Hamilton, the girls (everybody lumped Kerry and Alice together as "the girls,"

perhaps because they both are tiny and were nearly always together), Mattie Jo Arnold, and Mary Blackwell, a freshman music student from Athens who lived at home, formed a small society, seeing each other from time to time at Killian's during the week, transporting one another around Athens, and occasionally meeting at the home of a large Athens family to gossip and play bid-whist. Of the two other Negroes at the university, Harold Black, a freshman living in one of the men's dormitories, was rarely a member of the group, and Charlayne never.

When we returned to Killian's, I asked Hamilton about the Canterbury Club, the Episcopal student's organization, which, at the start of integration, had seemed to offer some possibilities as a home base. "I used to go to Canterbury every Wednesday, but I stopped going in the fall of last year," he said. "We used to go for services from five to five-thirty, and then we'd eat and there would be a program from seven to eight, and after that we'd play cards and that kind of thing. Everything was fine. We all talked and joked and everything. But the next day I'd see the same people on the campus and they'd turn their heads to keep from seeing me. It got so I couldn't take it. I almost blew up. I'd walk in that place and everybody would be smiling. It was just disgusting. Finally, I just couldn't take it any more and I left. I didn't say anything; I just never went back. After a month or so, the minister came up to check on me—because I had gone every Wednesday until then—and he asked me what was wrong and I told him. He said, 'Why don't you come back? Things will change.' I said, 'I don't want you to go back and tell the folks "Treat him nice." ' He thought it was his Christian duty to check up on me, but he wasn't too enthusiastic. I guess he figured he had done his duty to the Lord."

Hamilton's only other contact with campus organiza-

tions had been his initiation into Phi Kappa Phi, which
was friendly; two or three visits to Westminister House
for forums discussing integration; and a strange experience with a medical honorary society. "It's kind of unusual," he explained. "They don't tap you; you have to
make an application. The only qualification is an eighty-
three average, which is only a B average, and being a
junior and in pre-medicine. They initiate at the beginning
of every quarter. They asked me a few times if I was going to apply, so finally last fall I decided to fill out a card.
I was expecting to hear from them, and then a couple of
weeks later I saw that they had held their initiation. I
asked one of the boys about it and couldn't get any answer. But I was busy and I didn't push it. You know, they
haven't had any initiations since then—none last quarter, none this quarter so far. I put an end to that. Those
people are so stupid—all that trouble just to keep me out.
I wouldn't have pushed it; I wasn't going to bother with
it. But here they quit initiating anybody just to keep me
out. Those folks sure are stupid."

Hamilton said that on his own chosen field of combat,
the classroom, everybody had played by the rules and he
had no complaints about the instructors. "If anything,
they might have given me the benefit of the doubt," he
said. "One quarter last year I had a couple of instructors
I wasn't so sure about at first. They weren't too cordial. I'd see them on the street and they'd kind of frown
up. You know, in my position you get sensitive about such
things. But I found out they just weren't cordial types. I
got an A-plus out of one and an A out of the other, so I
don't guess they were holding me back. The students respect me in the classroom, but outside the classroom it's
a different thing altogether. I guess they think that outside the classroom I'm just another nigger. It used to

bother me. But all I can see now is June first. I'd sure like that Phi Beta Kappa key, but otherwise I'm just counting days. It was partly my fault, too. I'll admit I didn't try too hard. About this time last year I sort of gave up. I just figured I'd make it on my own. And, just so I can get home on the week ends, I'll make it."

Although Hamilton had often stressed that the atmosphere at Georgia would improve only if white students got used to seeing more Negroes around the campus, he had decided against trying to make himself a familiar sight. "Char wanted me to eat on campus, but it just didn't interest me," he said. "That just isn't in my personality. I would have been going out of my way, and I don't believe in that. At home I run with a few friends and my girl. It just wouldn't have been me to go down there to be noticed. I've concentrated on getting some good grades; I was so determined to show them that what they said about me wasn't true. I haven't gone out of my way at all to make friends. And I don't expect them to go out of their way—just go along in the normal way. I'm used to speaking to almost everybody I see. That's the way I was brought up. At home, when I walk down the street, I speak to almost everybody who passes. It's been that way all my life. All week I look up at people, wanting to speak, and people turn their heads. I guess that bothers me more than anything else."

I told Hamilton I had been having a hard time finding Harold Black, who never seemed to be in his room or at Westminster House, where Charlayne had told me he did his studying, and after dinner Hamilton suggested we drive over to Reed Hall, the dormitory where Harold lived. "Harold's an idealist," Hamilton said on the way. "I guess he had read about college life, and he thought he'd come here and have friends and do things. I told him, 'Slow

down, boy.' They tried to get me to talk him out of staying
in the dorm—Dean Tate did—and I did think it would be
better to wait until there were two boys to room together.
But he's stubborn. That boy's stubborn. He thought it
would be an ideal situation—playing cards with the boys
and all that. It's just not like that here now. Maybe a few
years from now, but not now."

When we arrived at Reed Hall, Hamilton walked casu-
ally through the lobby to Harold's room on the first floor.
He knocked, but Harold was still not home. The rest of
the doors in the hall had slatted panels in them, but
Harold's panel had been replaced by a solid piece of wood.
On it was scratched "Nigger Nest." Hamilton looked at it
and smiled. "That's just been put there since last quarter,"
he said. "I haven't seen it before. They had to take the
slats out and put this panel in because people were drop-
ping firecrackers through the slats. But Harold doesn't
complain. He won't even admit that anybody's bothering
him. That's one thing about that boy. Maybe it's because
he wants to show me that he was right about living in the
dorm, but he doesn't complain."

Hamilton and I drove back to Killian's. As I left his car,
I noticed that on the front bumper was a red and black
sign reading "Georgia Bulldogs." I had also seen Georgia
decals or bumper stickers on the cars driven by Charlayne and Mary Frances Early, and I asked Hamilton why
all the Negro students went in for such things. "Well, we
do go to school here," he said. "It's school—spirit? No, not
spirit. I'm trying to think of another word. I'll let you
know."

I was curious to learn how Harold Black had got into
the dormitory and how he was getting along there, and I
asked Dean Tate about it on one of my visits to his office.

He told me that he had offered to waive the rule that all freshman men must live on campus, since he felt, as Hamilton did, that a single Negro boy might still find it hard going in a freshman dormitory. When Harold declined the offer, he was given a room with no more fuss. "We do most things for this new boy," Tate said, "and I expect if pinch came to shove we would have done most things for Hamilton, too." He suggested that I talk to Dan Biggers, the head counselor for freshmen and the man directly in charge of the freshman dormitories, to find out how Harold was faring.

Biggers, a husky, straightforward Georgian in his mid-thirties, has his office in Reed Hall, and when I visited him there, he told me he was "mighty pleased and relieved" to see how well Harold had made out. "In many ways I think the boys believe it's a dead issue," Biggers said. "They just don't talk about it. There have been some incidents. There was some trouble with firecrackers, but that seems to have calmed down. And even at the time, nobody went around saying, 'Did you see what they did to him?' There's a bathroom near his room that could have been considered his own, but other people use it. It's no use pretending that a boy on the third floor could be as openly friendly with Harold as he could with anybody else and not get into some social complications. But Harold has friends. He isn't left to eat alone. We're not at the point of social acceptance, but we're going through a stage we have to go through to get there.

"Way back in the very beginning, the boys who were being overly friendly toward him were getting some pressure. I tried to caution them about being discreet, and I think it's worked out very well. Charlayne worried about him a lot at first; she used to call up here like a mother hen. Harold's done a lot of things that the others haven't.

He's gone to pep rallies for instance, and those are pretty lively events. He takes physical education. He's been to the campus movies. He even goes to a white church in town. Harold's extremely level-headed; he sees the big picture, and he's intelligent about it. There was a pep rally, by chance, the night after the bad trouble in Mississippi, and I thought it might not be a good idea for him to go to that one. I tried to call him to suggest that he skip it, and Charlayne called, worried that he would go. I finally reached him the next morning, and it turned out he had felt the same way and hadn't gone."

The attitude of Tate and Biggers seemed to the Negro students to be based on an honest interest in making the transition with as little disturbance as possible, which it was precisely their jobs to do. When Tate made a request —such as asking Hamilton, in the first weeks of integration, to postpone wearing his new University of Georgia windbreaker until tempers had cooled a bit—it was usually acceded to without question. But in dealing with some university officials, Hamilton and Charlayne must often have felt as if they were right back in the Athens federal court. What might in some hands have been a prudent means to an end became a stall that was meant to be an end in itself. University officials were sometimes so devious, so unwilling to discuss the problems presented by the Negro students directly, that it seemed as if they were afraid that Mrs. Motley or Hollowell would leap from the plaintiff's table in triumphant accusation if they mentioned the word "Negro" or "segregation."

For example, Harold Black was apparently the only Negro student who was treated honestly in the matter of dormitory space. Mary Frances Early had applied for a

single room after her first summer and had been told that
the space problem was precisely acute enough to neces-
sitate placing one graduate student in a freshman dormitory. Hamilton had thought briefly about moving onto
the campus and had applied for a room in a dormitory that
was mainly for law and graduate students but that also
had some room for senior honors students. "I went over
the first day you could apply and they said they were all
full," he told me. "Shoot, all full on the first day—I knew
that was a lot of baloney. But I wasn't that anxious to
move anyway, so I didn't push it."

Charlayne, trying to escape from an isolated room in a
freshman dormitory, did push it, and, after the most serious of her disagreements with the administration, was
still in Center Myers, the only senior there. The dean of
women's office, she said, had given several reasons for
refusing her another room: that Candler Hall, the dormitory she had requested, did not contain any single
rooms; that it did contain single rooms but none was available; that there was no way of knowing how the housemother in Candler would feel about having her there. At
one point, Charlayne became angry enough about the runaround to ask Hollowell to go back to court, but he decided
against it. Thinking it might be interesting to see what the
runaround was like, I decided to look into Charlayne's
rooming problem, starting with the office of the dean of
women.

Edith Stallings, the dean of women, turned out to be a
short, chubby lady who looked more like a housemother
than a dean and had a bubbling, cheerful style of conversation to match her appearance. Dean Stallings told
me that Charlayne was a fine girl and had "gotten along
just wonderfully." She seemed grieved at my bringing up
the unpleasant subject of room segregation, but the sub-

ject sounded much less unpleasant when she started talking about it.

"It's not a matter of segregation," she explained. "It's really more a matter of consideration. It's a kindness more than anything else not to put them into a dormitory where there's a gang bath and shower. I know a lot of parents would complain, and why hurt a girl that way? We don't like to put any student in a position where she's not wanted. It's not race. We have a problem with some of our own girls. We feel that if there's a conflict we can avoid we must try to avoid it. We wouldn't put a white student in such a situation. Why, we had a case where a little white girl was obnoxious, and the parents of another girl insisted they didn't want their daughter living with her, so we moved the little girl to another dormitory."

I reminded Dean Stallings that Charlayne was not obnoxious.

"Oh, no," she said, appearing shocked that I should even suggest such a thing. "Charlayne is a fine girl. She's gotten along just wonderfully."

Dean Stallings appeared to be a lady capable of finding a pleasant interpretation for the most heinous turn of events, and it seemed obvious that she was defending a decision somebody else had made. When I inquired about this, she said merely, "The decision didn't come from this office, but I think it's a good idea, and considerate."

The next step in the hierarchy was the dean of students, so I went to see Joseph Williams, with whom I had spent an uncomfortable hour or two in front of Center Myers Hall "that night." Since my last visit, Williams had been promoted to dean of the College of Education. In fact, he was often mentioned as a possibility for the university presidency after the retirement of O. C. Aderhold, an agricultural-education specialist, who had been dean

of the College of Education himself. Williams had still
been dean of students at the time Charlayne made her
room application, and he was quite certain that "when
she applied at Candler Hall it had been sold out—there
were no rooms available." I told him that Dean Stallings
had not mentioned a lack of space and had said that the
original decision did not come from her office, which
would certainly have had the authority to refuse an application if there was no room. "When I left the dean of
students' office in July, it was a matter of space," said
Williams. "After I left, I haven't inquired." Williams also
explained that Mary Frances Early had not actually been
denied permission to bring her family to a concert. "No
official exception was made," he said. "There was nothing
official about it. If she had insisted, she would not have
been denied permission. She was never told pointblank
that she couldn't bring anybody." Williams told me that
Negro students were no longer discouraged from bringing
guests onto the campus, and that Miss Early, in fact, had
invited an unusually large number of guests to her graduation ceremony.

Williams' behavior during the riot had been a subject
of fascination to reporters covering the desegregation of
the university, and I took advantage of my visit to ask him
how he had happened to make the decision to suspend
Charlayne and Hamilton—a decision he had insisted was
entirely his own. He talked about the danger of the mob,
and the danger to other students. Then he smiled and
said, "I knew they would be ordered right back in anyway."

A few days later I asked Williams' successor as dean of
students, Daniel Sorrells, whether Charlayne's room request had been denied for humanitarian reasons or because there was no room in Candler Hall. "Well," he said,

"it was really a combination of the two." I thought of asking why a combination was needed if there was no space,
but that line of questioning would probably have just
taken me right back to Dean Stallings.

"We could go back to court on the rooms," Donald Hollowell acknowledged when we met for lunch a few days
later on Hunter Street, in Atlanta. "But in the case of the
freshmen, university authorities would probably say that
they were put in Charlayne's suite not for purposes of segregation but so Charlayne could help them learn their
way around. It's obvious that she's being segregated in the
dorm, but it would be very difficult to prove. You would
have to balance any attempt against the added notoriety,
the added trouble and expense. We could probably prove
it. The question is: Is it worth it?"

Unlike most Southern cities, Atlanta does not have an
obvious scarcity of Negro lawyers. There are about two
dozen, as opposed to four in the entire state of Mississippi.
But some of them are not interested in civil-rights cases,
some of them ask as high a fee as the white lawyers on
the other side, some of them are incompetent—and most
of the civil-rights cases end up in Hollowell's office. It was
Hollowell who, a few weeks before, had requested the injunction ordering the removal of the roadblocks that had
become known as "Atlanta's Wall." He also had handled
the case to desegregate Atlanta's recreational facilities,
had been associate counsel on the Atlanta public-school
case, had handled the bus segregation cases in Atlanta,
Macon, and Augusta, and was associated in the suits to desegregate Georgia State and the Savannah public schools.
For a year or so, he had appeared continually in Atlanta
city court with sit-in demonstrators. While I was in Atlanta, he was busy trying to obtain a new trial for Preston

Cobb, Jr., a Jasper County Negro who became temporarily famous when he was sentenced to be executed for murder at the age of fifteen. Hollowell was also trying to maintain his own practice, and while he was going from court to court for Preston Cobb, in a successful attempt to stay the execution, he simply did not have time to desegregate Charlayne's dormitory.

"I was writing a lawyer today about how much time is consumed by cases of this kind," Hollowell said. "Just collateral time talking to the press, for instance." He had to end our lunch early. Some of the demonstrators I had seen in front of the Henry Grady Hotel on my first day back in Atlanta had been arrested when they refused to leave the lobby, and he had to be in court to defend them.

8

I HAD a chance to see Hamilton speak again the following
Saturday at the Forty-third Annual Dinner of the Phyllis
Wheatley Branch of the Y.W.C.A., a building on Hunter
Street, across from part of the Atlanta University campus.
Both Hamilton and Mary Frances Early spoke as members of a panel made up of Negro students who had entered previously all-white schools. The panel, whose
topic was "The Challenge of New Frontiers in Education," also included Willi-Jean Black, a senior at Northside
High School; Ford Greene, one of six Negro undergraduates at Georgia Tech; and Columbus Scott, who had been
admitted to Smith-Hughes Vocational School three
months before to study tool and die making. After dinner,
the program started with a prayer and responsive reading
led by Mrs. James Washington, an aunt of Hamilton's.
Then, after a series of reports and introductions, the

chairman presented the leader of the panel, a young psychiatrist from Boston named Robert Coles, who had just about completed a two-year study of Negro and white students in newly integrated schools, concentrating on the high-school students in Atlanta, where he had been living, and on the little girls who integrated the elementary schools of New Orleans. Dr. Coles did not have to do much prompting. After he had made some introductory remarks, the panel members passed the microphone around and spoke freely of their experiences. There was a great similarity in these experiences. Most of the speakers mentioned a gradual acceptance inside the classroom and a lingering coolness outside it. One or two said that the nastiest students they had encountered were from the North—people whom Dr. Coles described later as having "a high capacity for adjustment." Most of the panelists also mentioned the superiority of the facilities in their new schools, and—what struck them as even more important—a great difference in the attitude toward education from what they had known in Negro schools, whose atmosphere is often dominated by the realization on the part of both students and faculty that their ambitions are severely limited by the position of their race. As Ford Greene put it, "There is a distinct difference in students and teachers. The teachers are there to teach and the students are there to student."

Hamilton's speech was to the point, as usual, but it was angrier than anything I had ever heard him say in public before. "Basically, the things enumerated so far apply also to me," he began. "There are perhaps a few original contributions I can make to this discussion, so I'll go on out to that area and not bother with repeating. I want to get one point clear first. There's a tendency now with almost everybody I know in Atlanta not closely connected with me or the situation there to think that because Georgia isn't in the news everything is fine down there, and that I have buddies all over the campus, and we get no resistance. I'd like to clear that up right now. That is far from the case. Although there's not much said now, the atmosphere is just about the same as in January 1961. The only difference is that there is no overt resistance. The atmosphere is definitely an atmosphere of uncordiality. This is from a lack of responsibility on the part of both groups—white and Negro. It's partly our fault as a race. There should be ten, or fifteen, or even twenty times more Negro students at Georgia. Take in consideration the two and a half years we've been there. The second year, there weren't any applications. This year, we had six or seven people to be accepted, and they'd had to be just about drafted to apply. This is a big problem. It has bothered me, and I don't know how it can be overcome. I'm dumbfounded. But it *is* partly our fault and our responsibility that the atmosphere at Georgia is now what it is."

Hamilton went on to discuss the superior laboratory facilities at the new Georgia science center, concluding that, all in all, the whole miserable experience had probably been worthwhile because "I'm in sciences and I've been able to do experiments I would have never been able to do at Morehouse—also, probably, if I had stayed at Morehouse, I wouldn't have had a chance to go to Emory Medical School." The speech was not altogether what the audience had come to the Phyllis Wheatley dinner to hear, but Hamilton got a good round of applause when he finished.

One of the observations made in the panel discussion that interested me most was made by Columbus Scott, a stolid, heavy-set young man who was obviously most at home talking about tools and dies, and made no effort to simplify his language for an audience that was largely middle-aged ladies. "At first I got the silent treatment, more or less," he said when it was his turn at the microphone. "Nobody spoke. Then in the first class in my tool- and die-making course, my first task was to cut details of acme thread on a bronze lathe. On the first operation, I cut it to one ten-thousandth of an inch, which is very rare, especially on the first try. After that, I had more friends than I knew what to do with in the classroom."

What struck me about Scott's experience was that it corresponded so closely to the experiences of Hamilton and Charlayne. Hamilton had said that the students in his classes were always friendlier when he had made the highest mark on an exam or an experiment and Charlayne had found the same magic in Juvenal, the Latin satirist, that Scott had found in details of acme thread. "This classics class in summer school was real cold," she had told me the week before, in Athens. "Nobody would ever talk to me. And then I did this beautiful paper. It was pretty, if I do say so myself. And the teacher just ate it up. We had to do the paper on one person, and I was supposed to do it on Juvenal. I thought that instead of just giving name, rank, and serial number, I'd compare him with some people criticizing society today. There were a lot of similarities to some poems by Ferlinghetti, and I also brought in Motley's *Knock on Any Door* and Steinbeck's *Grapes of Wrath*. I showed we're the same as the degenerate Roman society." She laughed at the thought, and went on, "When I read it, everybody was real quiet. And right after that they started coming around and asking if they could read it, and from then on it was just amazing. Before, during the breaks I used to sit out on the stoop by myself and drink a Coke. But from then on somebody always came over to talk. It just happened all of a sudden. I've seen it warm up, but nothing like that. I wrote my mother about it; I just had to write it down. She read the letter to Carl [Holman] and he said the same thing had happened to him once at the Yale Drama School. Later, I started talking in class discussions, and this boy and I had a big argument about whether or not Dido should have thrown herself on a sword after Aeneas left Carthage. He said she had a responsibility to stay with her people instead, and I said she couldn't do her people any good because she didn't care about anything any more, so she might as well kill herself. Half the class sided with him and half with me. It was normal."

I suggested the possibility that a dazzling classroom performance might knock down the last myth propping up the prejudice of some white students—that of the innate mental inferiority of Negroes. "Well, the other time they warm up is when everybody flunks an exam and you flunk it too," Charlayne said. "Then they warm up even more."

Hamilton's speech at Phyllis Wheatley reflected a bitter realization, shared by Charlayne, that Atlanta Negroes were quick enough to get together and hand out plaques—Hamilton got one that night for his "contribution to Phyllis Wheatley"—but were often hard to corral when it came to formulating an organized program and establishing a scholarship fund to get more Negro students to go to the University of Georgia. Charlayne and Hamilton, who had assumed that there would be an influx of Negro students after their first year of loneliness, were extremely disappointed when not one applied for the following fall. Even during their last spring at Georgia, when it was too late for their own lives there to be affected, both of them constantly stressed the importance of getting more Negroes to attend the university.

Because a great number of Negro students did not immediately join Charlayne and Hamilton, the problem had become cyclical. The fewer Negro students there were at the university, the more unpleasant it was for those who were there, not only because they lacked company but because there was less opportunity to accustom white students to the presence of Negroes on the campus. And the more unpleasant it was for Negroes at the university, the fewer Negroes there were who wanted to go there. The cycle could be broken only by the arrival of a significant number of Negro students, and Jesse Hill, who is still more or less in charge of the search, thinks that this is unlikely. "I feel it will be years before there are a lot of Negro undergraduates there," he told me when I spoke to him in Atlanta. "Until the other cities start sending them, it will be mostly graduate students in the summer."

Even though the admission standards at the university are not high, most graduates of Negro high schools outside Atlanta cannot meet them, and no organizations have been formed to encourage the ones who can. In Atlanta, Hill restricts his search to A and B students, since he is convinced that only a student whom the university cannot turn down without risking another court case is likely to be accepted. Hill thinks that this is particularly true of male applicants, one of whom had been rejected the preceding fall despite what seemed to be reasonable marks on the college-board examinations and a good record at Turner.

In going after outstanding students, Hill runs into se-

vere competition. Atlanta Negroes have other practical
alternatives to the university besides the three state Negro colleges; those who are able to manage the tuition can
attend one of the private colleges of the Atlanta University Center, and live right at home. "An outstanding student can almost always get a full or partial scholarship to
a Negro school," Hill said. "Tech has something special
to offer, of course, but why should a person want to go
down to Athens?" If Georgia offers more academically
than even most of the private Negro colleges, it offers
considerably less socially. "I don't blame them for not going," Hamilton's mother told me. "It takes something out of
a kid. I've seen the wear and tear on Hamp." As compen-
sation for the wear and tear, a Negro who followed Charlayne and Hamilton to Georgia could not expect even the
plaques and adulation that they eventually found so hypo-
critical.

Hill is known in the Atlanta Negro community as a
catalyst rather than an administrator, and nobody has
come forward to organize the tedious and undramatic
business of sifting through records to find qualified students, battling the red tape at the admissions office, and
raising money for those students who need scholarships.
In the early days of integration, a group of whites and
Negroes who were interested in the problem held meetings in Atlanta and got as far as sending Negro high
schools in the state a pamphlet listing the courses offered
at the University of Georgia and outlining the procedure
for application. The pamphlet had no visible effects, however, and the group eventually broke up. While I was in
Atlanta, plans were being made to take advantage of an
approaching meeting of the Georgia Teachers Association, the state organization for Negro teachers, to talk to
teachers and counselors about encouraging students to
consider the University of Georgia, or at least to take the

college-board examinations required for admission. According to Hill, less than one per cent of the Negro high-school seniors in Atlanta take the college boards. Hill was also planning a campaign in the *Inquirer,* of which he is chairman of the board, on the advantages of going to Georgia and Georgia Tech.

Most of the time, all such activity seemed half-hearted. At one point, Hill did hold a meeting of the various Negro fraternal organizations in Atlanta, asking them to divert some of their funds into scholarships for students who were attending newly integrated colleges. The only group that agreed to do so was the Jack & Jills, a mothers' organization—and one whose president might have had an extra measure of sympathy with the project, since she was Mrs. Washington, Hamilton's aunt. The Jack & Jills began to support one of the freshman girls at Georgia. "In general," Hill told me, "we simply were not able to generate the kind of funds we expected." Because of this, the informal organization encouraging Negroes to go to Georgia has occasionally been in the position of implying that the community would take care of a scholarship for a prospective student, and then not being able to produce it when the time came. Mary Frances Early had needed some help, particularly for the spring quarter, when she took a leave of absence from her teaching job to attend Georgia. But when she was about ready to leave, the promised funds were still nowhere in sight. At the last minute, the Negro teachers in the Atlanta schools were asked to give two dollars apiece for a scholarship—an arrangement that was satisfactory neither to Miss Early nor to the teachers, some of whom grumbled that they were having enough trouble putting away a dollar here and a dollar there for the education of their own children.

The obvious solution to the problem would have been a scholarship fund, providing some steady source of aid and eliminating the need for a personal appeal on behalf of each student. Most people who have been concerned with the matter believe that the chance for a fund was lost as soon as the drama of the entrance and riot had faded from the front pages. "The difficulty with financing results from the fact that no one person or organization took the responsibility then and there," Hollowell told me. "A good fund could have been raised with the proper organization. I'm not thinking so much of Charlayne and Hamilton as of the people who came after them."

Even with Charlayne and Hamilton, the Student Heroes, money was always a problem. It had been assumed that the Negro community would provide an informal scholarship for the pioneers, whether they were in desperate need or not, and, particularly in Charlayne's case, some help was necessary. The plans, however, did not provide any method of maintaining financial support, and Charlayne's education was financed by a series of last-minute scramblings for cash. It was raised, Hill told me, "from quarter to quarter." Charlayne, who had assumed that whatever help she received would come from some sort of fund, resented having to make personal appeals. Sooner or later, she looked to Hollowell and Carl Holman, who—often the day before a new quarter began—scratched around Atlanta until they had got the money together.

While I was in Atlanta, I talked with one of the few people who had responded to Holman's last-minute appeals—Mrs. P. Q. Yancey, the wife of a doctor. The Yanceys live near Collier Heights, a Negro residential district that is always one of the first stops on any Chamber of Commerce tour of the city. (William B. Hartsfield, the retired mayor of Atlanta, liked to tell of Northern journalists who refused to believe that Negroes lived in its forty-thousand-dollar houses until the mayor went to the door to prove who lived there—and even then, Hartsfield said, the journalists weren't convinced because they concluded that the Negro who answered the door was probably the butler.) Mrs. Yancey's large house is set back from the street, in grounds that include a private tennis court. One of her sons was at Villanova, she told me, and another at a prep school in Massachusetts. Her third son was the first Negro to attend Marist, a Catholic military school in Atlanta, where one of Charlayne's brothers had just been accepted.

Because many of the Atlanta Negroes interested in Charlayne and Hamilton live, if not quite as grandly as Mrs. Yancey, at least in middle-class comfort, it is not always easy for people to remember the simple fact that underlies the need for fund-raising—that very few Negroes can afford to send their children to college. Mrs. Yancey, who seemed to have no trouble remembering this, had some unkind words for her neighbors. "This is a selfish community," she told me. "Oh, they'll give to the United Negro College Fund or the N.A.A.C.P.—their consciences make them do that—but they've been too busy too long trying to get things for their own families to worry about other people.

"Carl Holman called me one day and said, 'That girl can't go back to school unless we get some money.' A friend of mine here knew a man in Memphis who is in charge of the Negro Elks education fund, and she called him, and within two or three days we had some help. It wasn't all we wanted, but we had something. We also managed to get something from a women's club that had some money sent down from an organization to be used for the student sit-ins or a similar project. Since we were already raising money for the sit-ins, I managed to get the money for Charlayne, although it wasn't as easy as I thought it would be. Then I asked my husband one day— he belongs to two clubs, exclusive clubs, of businessmen and professionals—'What are you doing, all you rich men?' Of course, they're not *really* rich. He managed to raise money at both of the clubs. But we missed the psychological time. Right at the start, when everybody in the country was interested, we should have organized something, the way we did for the sit-ins right when the demonstrations were going on. I hope Charlayne isn't bitter, but I think she is, a little. She felt that it should have come easier, and she was right."

Charlayne received a check for eighty-three dollars from the Elks at the beginning of each quarter, the total of two hundred and forty-nine dollars for the academic year constituting her only steady income. Minimum expenses for a year at Georgia, according to Charlayne's estimates, amounted to between thirteen hundred and fifteen hundred dollars, and much of the difference was made up through such gifts as a United Packinghouse Workers scholarship for five hundred dollars; room and tuition payments for one quarter by Delta Sigma Theta, the sorority she had joined at Wayne; a check from an organization of postal workers in Atlanta; and the honorariums that she and Hamilton ordinarily received for their speeches.

The irony of the Student Heroes' being unable to get scholarships was heightened by the belief among University of Georgia undergraduates that Charlayne and Hamilton were being paid generously by the N.A.A.C.P. Fifty thousand dollars was usually the figure mentioned, though some people believed it was fifty dollars a day, which, for two and a half academic years, works out to be considerably less. As a matter of fact, the N.A.A.C.P. is one organization that has a policy of not giving even an occasional honorarium. "There's a plaque in our den from the N.A.A.C.P.," Charlayne told me one day. "That's what I got from them, exactly." Even so, neither Charlayne nor Hamilton did much to discourage the N.A.A.C.P. story. Charlayne said that after a football scandal broke at Georgia as the result of an alleged overheard telephone conversation, "This boy came up to me in class and said, 'It's the funniest thing—a lady in my home town called my mother last week and said that she was on the phone and heard you talking to the N.A.A.C.P. in Jacksonville, asking for more money. Isn't that funny?' I told him, 'Yeah, buddy, that's pretty funny.' I guess he expected me to deny it."

Charlayne's car was often pointed to by undergraduates as an example of her heavy financing by the N.A.A.C.P. Some of them felt that their case was proved when Mary Frances Early showed up with a compact car of the same model and even the same color, indicating the possibility of purchase in wholesale lots. "They wondered why Hamp's was different," says Miss Early, "and we told them they have a different color for boys." The cars were also used as an excuse by Negroes in Atlanta for not supporting the students financially. Many of them, said Charlayne, had heard the N.A.A.C.P. story so often that they had come to believe it themselves; others thought anybody who could afford a car at college had no need of a scholarship. Hamilton's car was a gift from his grandfather. Charlayne's mother had borrowed the money to buy Charlayne's car, believing that on an unfriendly 260-acre campus it might well be a necessity rather than a luxury.

Mrs. Yancey had suggested that I talk to Hamilton's aunt, Mrs. Washington, and on the day after the Phyllis Wheatley program I drove back to Mrs. Yancey's neighborhood, where the Washingtons live in a pleasant brick house. When I arrived, Oliver Wendell Holmes, who is a bachelor and lives with his sister and brother-in-law, was about ready to leave for his Sunday-afternoon golf game. I had heard that Holmes helped Columbus Scott, the tool-and-die student, in his effort to get into Smith-Hughes Vocational School, and I asked him just how difficult that had been in the new atmosphere in Georgia.

"Yessir, that's my boy," Holmes said proudly. Scott, he told me, had graduated from Turner two or three years before Charlayne and Hamilton. He spent five years in the Army, during which he became interested in tool-and-die work and even attended a German civilian school in the subject for a while. When he got back to Atlanta, he went to Carver, the Negro vocational school, to take a tool-and-die course and was told that none was available for him in the city. Scott worked in another field until one day he answered an advertisement for a tool-and-die apprentice. He was informed that only Smith-Hughes graduates were hired. That put Scott in the desegregation business, Holmes said, although he was actually interested only in taking a tool-and-die course.

"Scott filed application for Smith-Hughes," Holmes went on, "but the night principal told him to see the day principal and the day principal said, 'Why, I don't know why he would send you to me; that's a matter for the night principal.' And he started to get the old runaround." Scott's mother was a friend of the secretary in the office of the Georgia Council on Human Relations, and she asked if the Council could help. After making certain that Scott realized what he might be getting into, Holmes accompanied him to Smith-Hughes and saw on the bulletin board that the tool-and-die course was offered in both the day and night sessions. (Holmes later published a report listing seventeen subjects that were offered at Smith-Hughes and not at Carver.)

"We went to see the principal again," Holmes said, "and he said we should go over to Carver, because they're now offering the course. The principal at Carver is just as friendly as he can be; he's been waiting to see us. He tells us that Carver is going to offer the course, beginning in January, and later they had a big meeting, with all the leading lights of the Negro community, and the leading-light whites, and they showed this hundred and fifty thousand dollars' worth of new equipment and told about all their great plans, and everybody's happy again. Well, I asked Scott, 'What are you going to do?' He said he would just as soon go to Carver, so he was going to wait three months until January. Jimmy Washington here first let the cat out of the bag when he came in one night and said, 'I met a fellow who's going to be one of the teachers at the tool-and-die-making course at Carver and he can't even *spell* tool. He might be a carpenter, but probably not even that.' So I sent Scott out to Carver to see what the equipment looked like and to write up a report. Well, he came back and said the equipment was useless. It couldn't run. It had no component parts, none were on order, and the professor wouldn't know how to order them anyway. And the ground wasn't level and there wasn't even any electricity. So we went back to Smith-Hughes and told them what Scott found out. We finally got to see the deputy superintendent, who hadn't answered Scott's letters before, and he started talking about the dimly lighted corridors and the dimly lighted parking area, and we said, 'That's not our problem. That's a police problem.' Well, he said, the city is going to spend six million dollars for a new industrial school in three years and they were thinking about three million for white and three million

for Negro, but if there were no disturbing incidents between now and then, maybe they would just build one
school for the six million. Well, I said, 'That's a fine idea,
but meanwhile what's this boy supposed to do for three
years, go and hide?' Well, the deputy superintendent said
he's going to have a breakfast meeting with the superintendent and everybody, and they're going to talk about it.
Finally he called and said, 'When can you have your
boy over here to register?' And I said, 'Oh, ten or fifteen
minutes.' This whole business took about three months.
The school board announced Scott's registration, and the
newspapers wrote about how nice it was that everything
had been done voluntarily. You couldn't help but laugh."

Mrs. Washington is also involved with the admissions
problem, as a teacher-counselor in the Fulton County
school system. "The counselors in Negro schools have
hesitated to recommend white colleges in the past," she
said. "They've been afraid of their jobs. But that's less
true now. Ford Greene's mother has been made a principal since Ford went to Tech, and I don't think there
has been any pressure against Isabella, Hamilton's
mother. In fact, during the sit-ins, one high-school principal used to leave word occasionally in his office that he
was down bailing his daughters out of jail. Times are
changing."

Times, however, still have a long way to go as far as
the Washingtons are concerned. James Washington, a
Morehouse man who often joins his brother-in-law and
father-in-law for U.G.A. golf tournaments, works as a
mail carrier at the Atlanta post office. "The University of
Georgia is still like any place else here," said Washington. "To be accepted, the Negro has to be super-special.
It's the same at the post office. All but two or three of the
Negroes there have been to college, and most of us have
graduated from college."

Even if the University of Georgia gave no thought whatever to the question of race and made a conscious effort to treat all citizens alike—sending its admissions representatives to Negro high schools as well as white ones, for example, and removing the designation of race from its applications—there would be few Negro students on the campus, although real or suspected prejudice might influence the number of Negroes who think they have a chance of being accepted if they try. Some Georgia faculty members, who were dismayed by the way university officials lent themselves in court to the Ritual, are afraid that the prejudice might be real enough. When I told one of them that I was going to ask Walter Danner, the registrar, about the admission of Negroes, he said, "In a way, the key to the Administration's behavior is whether they're playing it straight now."

Danner told me that he formally admitted all students, but that his role in admitting graduate students was more or less nominal, since it consisted of giving official approval to their application on the recommendation of the admissions committee and dean of the graduate school. Freshmen, he said, were admitted according to a standard mathematical formula, which combined the applicant's high-school record and his college-board aptitude scores to predict the grade average he would have at Georgia. Everybody above a certain predicted average was taken, and the borderline cases were turned over to the admissions committee. The minimum for males living in the state, the committee's chairman told me later, was that year a predicted average of 68, or D, slightly higher minimums being required for female applicants and for applicants who did not live in Georgia. Using this system, Danner had sent admission notices to 2495 freshmen the previous fall and had rejected 285. For that class, four Negroes were accepted and five rejected. All five, he said, were rejected strictly on grades and college-board results. No case had to be settled by the admissions committee, and no one had been turned down on the basis of a pre-admission interview as Hamilton had been. After the court ordered Hamilton into the university, the admissions specialists seemed to have lost interest in interviews. When I told Danner that some people in Atlanta suspected him of bias, he assured me that Negroes "are considered right with the other students." Any other answer was, of course, unlikely. In two different court cases during the years Georgia was bragging about its segregation, Danner had sworn that his office had not discriminated against Negroes.

The professor whom I had spoken to earlier agreed that the disparity in the percentage of white and Negro applicants accepted could as easily be the result of a difference in qualifications as the result of prejudice. And he had an admissions story of his own. A Negro graduate student, a young woman, had applied for the summer session in his department, he said. Her application was brought up in a faculty meeting with the other applications, discussed routinely, approved, and sent to Danner for action. Her race was clear only through the name of her undergraduate college. The professor said he was amazed at how simple the whole problem suddenly seemed—a graduate student's being accepted on the basis of her record. Then he added, "I guess that's what this is all about."

On the surface, it might seem that the ten thousand Negroes who live in Athens had benefited most from the University of Georgia's integration, since it afforded their young people the opportunity of getting a reasonably good education without leaving home—a bargain of the sort that has been responsible for the educations of thousands of Americans who happened to live in college towns. Yet there was only one Negro student from Athens at Georgia—Mary Blackwell, a small, shy Music Department freshman who was the oldest of ten children of an Athens taxi driver. In many ways, her life seemed less different from what it would have been if she were white than that of any other Negro student at Georgia. The contrast between Hamilton's life as a football hero at Morehouse and as an alien at Georgia was obvious, but Mary Blackwell's routine did not seem to vary greatly from that of any poor, shy college-town girl who was managing to get an education she would otherwise have missed. When I spoke to her one evening in the library of the Music Department, she said she sang in the chorus and played flute in an orchestra made up of students, faculty, and musically inclined Athenians. Although she found the general atmosphere on the campus hostile, and preferred to drive with Mattie Jo Arnold to a self-service hamburger stand for lunch rather than try a university dining hall, her life in the Music Department was not unpleasant. As a music-education major specializing in piano, she spent most of her time there, and, she said, "They seem to be used to seeing me." Mary particularly liked the other piano students, who gathered once a week at their professor's studio, and she had found the faculty uniformly fair and thoughtful. She laughed as she recalled the only disturbing incident that had taken place in the Music Department. "Our practice rooms are downstairs, and that was before we had venetian blinds, so you could see right into them from the street through big windows," she said. "I used to practice from five to seven-thirty, and there's usually nobody here then, or maybe one or two people upstairs. One night—it was a practical joke, I guess—this boy barged through the door with a scarf over his face and a toy pistol in his hand and screamed, 'Bang, bang.' It was just a joke, but it scared the life out of me. He almost knocked over another girl as he was running out. After that, the head of the Music Department decided that I shouldn't be here alone, and he arranged for me to practice in the mornings between classes."

One reason there were not more Negro students from Athens at Georgia was money. Mary's education was being financed mainly by a local Veterans of Foreign Wars post, but the opportunities for outside financing in Athens are limited, and the number of Negroes who can afford even the low in-state tuition is small. More important, practically none of the Negroes who are both willing and financially able to go to the university could get in. Charlayne and Hamilton had wanted to go to court about one boy from Atlanta who had been rejected, since they were convinced that he was qualified (because the boy himself was not enthusiastic about a court case, and Hollowell was busy defending Preston Cobb, the boy ended up at Morehouse), but nobody in Athens complained about prejudice in the rejection of three Athens Negroes who had applied for admission to the same class, because nobody in Athens pretends that the town's Negro high school, Athens High and Industrial, could conceivably produce more than one or two students able to meet the relatively undemanding minimum requirements for admission to the University of Georgia.

I had heard that Athens High and Industrial started offering geometry only two or three years before, and when I called on the Clarke County school superintendent, Sam Wood, at the old Victorian house that the Clarke County school board uses as its headquarters, this was one of the first things I asked him about. After a quick phone call to Professor H. T. Edwards, the principal of Athens High and Industrial, Wood told me that the recent addition was advanced algebra rather than geometry. A survey of Athens education by the League of Women Voters the previous fall had, I knew, listed twenty-six courses that were still offered only at Athens High, the white high school, among them American government, physical science, trigonometry, Latin, Spanish, German, and art. The main difference between the two schools—and the reason that most Athens High seniors score between 350 and 500 on the college boards, while any Athens High and Industrial student who takes the exams usually scores less than 300—does not lie in the curriculum, however.

Since Athens has no significant Negro middle class, most Negro students start out at a cultural disadvantage relative to the white students, many of whom are children of college professors. The Negroes may also have a psychological disadvantage, in a society that offers them few job opportunities, no matter what their education, and calls their principal "Professor," one of the titles that were originally used in the South as a way of recognizing a position without going so far as to call a Negro "Mister." But mostly, according to Wood, the difference lies in the teaching. Athens High and Industrial, he said, had a teaching staff that was qualified "only on paper," and, despite some in-service training programs, it was still woefully behind. Although Athens had shown more interest than most Georgia towns in improving Negro education, its Negro children remained caught in the cycle of half-educated teachers teaching students who, in turn, became half-educated teachers—an educational cycle that could only be broken by integration, whatever the social and political ramifications of that might be.

As I was leaving Wood's office, he told me of a conversation he had recently had with Professor Edwards.
"I told Professor Edwards I wasn't taking up for segregation or anything," he said, "but, just forgetting for a
minute the sociologists and the Supreme Court and politics and all that, didn't he think his people were better off
right now—maybe not later but right now—in their own
schools? I said, 'Remember last year when I came out to
your school to induct ten of your seniors into the National
Honor Society? Now, just how many of those seniors do
you think would have made the National Honor Society
at Athens High—with that competition?' And he said,
'Not the first one.' " If the goal of education is a wider
distribution of National Honor Society places, Wood had a
good point, but it was probably lost on the Negro seniors
who made the National Honor Society and found themselves with so little education that they could not be given
a predicted average of 68 at the University of Georgia.

"If they figure the Negro kids in Atlanta are about two
years behind by the time they're seniors," Carl Holman
once remarked to me, "you can imagine how far behind
the ones in the rest of the state are." Even in Atlanta
(where most of the Negro undergraduates at Georgia
Tech, all of whom had been outstanding students in Atlanta Negro high schools, were having academic diffi-
culties), the situation is not likely to change soon. The
Atlanta desegregation program is based on integrating
one grade a year, starting with high-school seniors and
moving down, and with the Negro transfer students accepted on the basis of an elaborate pupil-placement plan
that requires certain standards of intelligence, psychological fitness, and educational background. The pupil-
placement plan, which nowhere mentions race, is "not on

its face unconstitutional," according to court rulings so far, and it is generally used to hold down the number of Negroes entering white schools. Some Negro leaders have no objection to gradual integration plans, provided they represent a sincere effort to break the cycle without pulling down what education there is. The Atlanta plan, however, has nothing to do with education. Instead of beginning in the first grade, where white and Negro students can make an almost equal start, and phasing in the Negro students from the bottom up, it begins in the twelfth grade—where the disparity, having been fostered by twelve years of inferior education, is strongest—and goes backward, each class finding the transition from inferior education slightly less agonizing, until, after a dozen years, the program ends up where it should have started in the first place. The advantage of such a plan, in the eyes of some politicians, is that fewer Negroes are likely to be involved in the first year or two of integration, since few seniors can meet the pupil-placement requirements. They are unqualified precisely because of the inequality that the 1954 decision was meant to correct. According to its present desegregation plan, Atlanta, which was widely praised in 1961 for its peaceful compliance with the 1954 decision, will not start a Negro student on an equal footing with whites until 1971.

9

ONE morning during my second week in Athens, I met Charlayne and Hamilton outside their philosophy class, which, as it happened, was the first course they had taken together since enrolling at Georgia. They were both reading the new issue of the *Red and Black*. Three letters from graduate students and instructors had been published in reply to the column calling Hamilton an alien, and all the letter-writers took sarcastic exception to the columnist's complaints that Hamilton was merely a serious student and took no part in extracurricular activities. "Look at this one here," Hamilton said. "I think this guy is our philosophy lecturer." The last sentence of that letter said, "To be a Negro is bad enough, but to be an intelligent Negro is unpardonable." Both Hamilton and Charlayne seemed greatly cheered by the letters.

The casualness with which they had applied for admis-

sion to a university that was likely to treat them as aliens
—a casualness that still amazes Jesse Hill—was explained to me by Hamilton a few days later. "I guess being first, the novelty of it, had something to do with it,"
Hamilton said. "But it was just something to do. If anybody had told me I would ever be here, I would have
laughed. I didn't have the slightest idea I would ever come
down here. They hadn't done anything like that in the
South." After all, Horace Ward, the first Negro to apply
to Georgia, had spent years in court without ever seeing
the Georgia campus. Although the University of Georgia
had seemed like a tempting challenge to both Charlayne
and Hamilton, not even Hamilton, who brought up the
idea, had seriously believed that all the commotion would
end up in their attendance there.

When they did consider the realities of being at Georgia, both had underestimated how long the unfriendli-
ness would last. Neither had ever experienced constant
hostility. Although Charlayne spent her early childhood
in her mother's home town of Covington, not far from
Athens, she had often lived on or near an Army base, and
had sometimes spent summers with relatives in New
York. Hamilton had faced the limitations of a Negro in
the South, it is true, but nowhere are those limitations
better camouflaged than in the nearly self-sufficient Negro community of Atlanta—especially for an outstanding member of a prominent family. In Atlanta, Hamilton
had indeed said hello to everybody he saw on the street,
because almost everybody he saw on the street was a
Negro who knew him. Both he and Charlayne had been
remarkably successful at Turner High School, and at
graduation they had had the optimism of seventeen-year-
olds who had just conquered their world. Could any students fail to be charmed sooner or later by the engaging

girl who had been named Miss Turner? Could people fail
to respect Hamilton's abilities as an athlete and a student?
"I really thought it would be broken down after two and a
half years," Hamilton admitted. "It was nice to see those
letters in the *Red and Black,* and several people came up
to me in class about it. It was nice to see people speaking
out. But it's a little late. We're about ready to leave."

Charlayne had been even more optimistic than Hamilton. "I thought there would be a coolness for a couple of
weeks," she told me, "but I never thought it would last for-
ever, and in some ways it has." It amazed me to discover
that the warnings that Charlayne and Hamilton had received from Carl Holman and Whitney Young as to what
a Negro could expect at Georgia had failed to puncture
their teen-age euphoria. Most of the other Negro students
I had met in the South had been in sit-in movements; they
had had a fierce consciousness of their role, and a knowledge that they would get no better treatment from whites
than they demanded. Moreover, the report of Dr. Coles,
the Boston psychiatrist, stressed the fact that the nine
Negro teen-agers who integrated the Atlanta public
schools in the fall of 1961—while they were relatively un-
informed on other aspects of current affairs—had a detailed and graphic knowledge of race incidents; for example, they had a vivid recollection of watching the Little
Rock mobs on television, even though they were only
about eleven at the time.

But the burning interest in civil rights among Negro
students, Charlayne told me, had started quite suddenly in February 1960, after the first sit-in in Greens-
boro, North Carolina. She reminded me that there had
been no previous indications of student unrest, and that
students had certainly not always been in the forefront
of the integration movement. Negro students in the South

might have increasingly resented not being able to have a Coke in a place where they were spending their money for other goods, but before 1960 they showed no sign of believing they could do anything about the situation themselves. That was the period when Jesse Hill, looking for a breakthrough at Georgia State, could find no candidates of college age and had to confine himself to older people who might be able to go to the night school.

Charlayne and Hamilton were twelve when the Supreme Court ruled segregation unconstitutional, fourteen when Autherine Lucy briefly attended the University of Alabama, fifteen when United States paratroopers were ordered into Little Rock. Charlayne said that when she and Hamilton first applied to Georgia in 1959—before the Greenboro sit-in—they had no strong recollection of those events. "What people don't realize," she went on, "is that the sit-ins happened all of a sudden and nobody talked about the problem before then. For instance, after we applied, people said, 'Keep your mouth shut; that's how they got Autherine Lucy.' So I thought, Okay, I'll keep my mouth shut and I won't end up like Autherine Lucy. Negro kids in Atlanta don't read the papers. Kids in Detroit were more interested in civil rights than we were; at least they talked about it more. I never thought much about a commitment to civil rights until the summer of 1960, when I got back from my freshman year at Wayne and all my buddies were going to jail. That's when I started writing for the *Inquirer*. I wanted to go to jail too. I thought that what I was doing, even if it might be just as important eventually, was not active enough. But I told Wilma at the time, 'Isn't it funny that things like this never really mattered to us until now?' Not one tenth of one per cent of those kids in the sit-ins gave a rap about the whole business before then." Wilma Long, one of

Charlayne's closest friends in Atlanta, is the daughter of
the high-school principal Mrs. Washington had mentioned
—the man who occasionally had to leave school during
the sit-ins to bail his daughters out of jail.

"For that brief period of time, I got interested in the
Cause," Charlayne said. "But now I'm fed up with causes.
I'm not here for any cause. I can't even say it's my contribution, as some people say. I'm just here because I'm
here. It was an interesting thing to do, and, after Wayne,
I figured I'd started it so I'd finish it. Maybe it would have
been better if Hamp and I had just come to Georgia cold
instead of going somewhere else first. We wouldn't have
known what we were missing. But this way I guess we got
a little bit of college life we wouldn't have had otherwise."

There was little evidence that Charlayne was really
fed up with the Cause. She had continued to write arti-
cles for the *Inquirer,* often on such subjects as overcrowded conditions in segregated schools; she had met
with Negro high-school students in Atlanta to encourage
them to apply for transfers to white schools; and she
often expressed her admiration of what was being done
by people like Constance Motley. But she *was* fed up with
talking about the Cause, or being considered its personifi-
cation. She disliked conversations that dwelt on her role
as one of the first Negroes at Georgia, and anybody who
offered her advice on how one of the first Negroes should
act or presented her with a careful plan for desegregating
a university facility was almost certain of being put down
in her book as a "goody-goody."

By the start of her last quarter at Georgia, Charlayne's
closest friend on the faculty was Joseph Schwarz, a young
art professor who, the day after the riot, had been one of
the organizers of the faculty resolution that called for the
reinstatement of Charlayne and Hamilton. "Out of all the

people who prepared that resolution, Joe Schwarz was the only one who didn't have tenure," she said. "That took a lot of guts. But he didn't make a big thing out of it. Some of these people have been living on that resolution ever since they passed it. But he just did it. He doesn't talk about it as if he were a hero." Schwarz and Charlayne, both perhaps wary of being a goody-goody, did not come to know each other until Charlayne had been at Georgia for a year and a half. Then one of her friends, a graduate art student who had been in the Students for Constructive Action, told Charlayne that Schwarz would like to do her portrait, and eventually they met. "We had more fun the first day I sat," Charlayne said. "We both felt we had to talk about the Issue, but we just wanted to get it out of the way, so we could talk about other things. And I didn't mind talking about it. He told me a lot of things I hadn't known about how the professors got up the resolution and everything, and he didn't make a big thing out of it. It's funny. My mother had kept mentioning this gray-haired lady who was at the trial and was so nice and had said she was a professor's wife. And I didn't find out until last month, when I went over there for dinner, that the lady was Mrs. Schwarz, who is prematurely gray."

Although many of Charlayne's friends were active at Westminster House, she was not attracted by the race-relations discussions that were held there during her first year by the Reverend Hardin W. (Corky) King. "Everybody over there talked as if everything was all good or all bad," she said. "They kept making statements that started with 'you people.' There is a lot of Cause talk that I don't believe in, and I just never felt I could be a human being over there. I told them I get tired of causes, and they were shocked. They always have to have these elaborate plans of attack; nothing is dramatic enough otherwise. I didn't figure I was adding much to the discussion and I felt much better when I left. As long as people make you out to be a perfect person, it's hard to be a perfect person. Our being here is a great thing; it must be. But some things about it aren't great, and it's silly to pretend they are."

Charlayne's experience with the Newman Club, the campus Catholic organization, was also unsatisfactory. "It was kind of phony," she said. "Well, not phony, but there was nothing for me to do. For one thing, a lot of people were there to find a girl friend or a boy friend, and they kind of paired off. I danced with white boys a couple of times at parties, and it wasn't exactly a hit. They were going to have another party, and it was at a private club, and there was talk about whether I would want to go. I wasn't going to go, and cause them any trouble, but I do think they could have had the party someplace where I *could* go. Then, the first fall, there was this boy from New York who was running for secretary—one of the food-technology boys—and he asked would I be his campaign manager. I asked the priest did he think I would hurt the boy's chances, and he said no, so I did it. I spoke more on the principles of Newmanism than on the boy's qualifications, because he didn't really have any. But anyway, he won. I'd told him I would have to meet with him before the speech, to learn something about him, so he said, 'Let's meet in the dining hall for dinner.' He started eating dinner with me every night; I would come in about six o'clock and he would come over to my table. One day my adviser in the dean's office called me and said she'd heard I was dating a white boy and she didn't think it was a good idea. I told her I wasn't dating any white boys, but he stopped having dinner with me anyway. I think he was under a lot of pressure—threats and things. I got the impression he'd been looking for trouble. For instance, he would make smart remarks to the other boys as we left the dining hall. He left a note in my car one day apologizing for not being able to see me any more. I saw him later and told him I thought the note was childish. Maybe that wasn't fair; I couldn't really blame him. But I just don't have any sympathy for people who ask for trouble and then can't take it."

Charlayne, unlike Hamilton, had a few white friends at Georgia from the beginning. Mostly journalism or graduate students, some of them were from Atlanta or the North, but some of them were from rural Georgia. By and large, they were students who were not greatly concerned with the social pressure exerted by fraternities and sororities. The more overt forms of pressure, such as the threats received by her friend in the Newman Club, were not common, especially after the first year or so. None of Charlayne's friends hesitated to have lunch with her on the campus or go with her to a university play, and the fact that Charlayne and a white boy often ate lunch together and rode around the campus together late in her senior year caused no serious commotion among the students. "It's hard to tell whether they're just more used to it or there's a degree of acceptance," one of Charlayne's friends, Joan Zitzelman, told me. "People are a little more polite this year, maybe. Maybe fewer remarks are made. I think more people are willing to know her on a personal basis. Last year, she was still the Negro Student. And I think people who associate with her do not have as much to lose as they did last year. But it's really hard to tell." Many of Charlayne's friends were students who, like Joan Zitzelman, had belonged to the Students for Constructive Action, were active in Westminster House, and had been friendly from the start. Although

some well-connected fraternity and sorority people were
perfectly civil to Charlayne in class and on the campus,
most of the people who ate lunch with her or rode around
Athens with her or visited her in Atlanta were, in the
words of one professor, "not the people in the mainstream."

Since the number of places where Charlayne and her
friends could go together was limited, they often ended up
in the coffee shop of the Continuing Education Center.
"Sometimes we just ride around and around because
there's no place to stop," Charlayne told me. "The social
scene is bad. I always have somebody to eat with and
talk to, but there are limits. The times I feel most like an
'alien' is when they have a journalism conference at C.E.
and afterwards the journalism students break up and go
to parties and I can't go. It's not as if I were an agriculture student; I'm a journalism student. Maybe Hamp's
way is better. He just doesn't get involved. It's more frus-
trating for me, in a way. I get so involved that sometimes
I get to thinking I'm human."

Tommy Johnson, the business manager Charlayne had
worked for, briefly, on the *Red and Black,* was one of the
few students in the Journalism School who qualified as a
big man on campus, having been the secretary-treasurer
of both his junior and his senior class, the president of
Sigma Nu, one of the leading fraternities, the commander
of the University's R.O.T.C. battalion, and a member of
all the most desirable honor societies. A tall, crew-cut boy
from Macon, Johnson was at Georgia on a scholarship
from his home-town paper, and I had first met him in the
early days of integration, when he was helping the Macon
News reporter cover the story. Since he seemed to be in a
good position to assess student opinion—which, I realized,

was probably a product of the minority at Georgia—I
stopped in at his office at the *Red and Black* one evening
to ask him whether the column calling Hamilton an alien
was typical of what most students thought.

"I guess it is," Johnson said. "The students have accepted the fact that the two of them are here—at least
they're not opposing it by physical means—but they're
not one of the group. I don't think they'll ever be accepted
in the social ring. At every Southern university, there
will always be a hard core holding out against them. But,
by and large, there's an apathetic attitude. Besides, people looked at Mississippi and saw that what happened
there really brought a lot of discredit on the institution.
At the start of the quarter you do hear, 'How many this
quarter?' People realize that they have the right to come
here, but they resent that they're here. There's a tendency
for students to say, 'I don't want to sit beside her,' because of what their friends might say. I don't have any
hesitation about stopping and talking to Charlayne in the
hall; I've done it several times. And a lot of people say
hello on the campus."

When I remarked that Charlayne still heard abusive
remarks on the campus, Johnson seemed quite surprised.
I asked him what would happen if, because of some common interest, he might decide to have lunch with Hamilton Holmes, and he said, "I'd be ostracized pretty much.
There would be numerous criticisms. There's an attitude
of apathy toward their being here, but there's no real acceptance. I guess it's just the way we were all brought
up."

Johnson nodded when I said I'd gathered that any student—white or Negro—who didn't belong to a fraternity
or sorority was not in the mainstream of the university's
social life. "Your Interfraternity Council dominates the

campus here," he told me. "It's the most powerful body. Every major officer is a Greek—the president of your senior class, the president of the student body. It seems like your top-quality people are Greeks."

Later that week I met some of the top-quality people and some of the hard core at the same time, as a result of having suggested to Johnson that it might be instructive for me to spend an hour or two chatting with his fraternity brothers. Sigma Nu is a fraternity with strong small-town domination. When Hamilton spoke of "crackers," he often mentioned the Sigma Nus just after such fraternities as the dependably hostile A.T.O.s and, of course, the flag-flying Kappa Alphas. ("They don't even take that flag in when it rains," Hamilton often said. "What a bunch of crackers!") The undergraduate who cast the first brick into Charlayne's room on the night of the riot was a Sigma Nu; he had later been suspended for his part in the riot and had been reinstated after a quarter's suspension. On the other hand, one of the fraternity's most famous alumni, Senator Herman Talmadge, had been quite cordial when Charlayne, out of curiosity, dropped in to see him during a visit to Washington the previous fall.

In any event, the Sigma Nus who gathered around me in their living room late one night seemed, despite their rush-party kind of friendliness, as firmly determined to prove that they were segregationists as the law students had been two and a half years before. (One of the law students had told me, "The long arm of judicial tyranny is crushing us under the heel of its boot.") It seemed obvious that they could not always have displayed as much emotion when the subject came up; otherwise they would have worn each other out in a month or two. Their opinions were a menagerie of clichés: there was the conspiracy of the N.A.A.C.P., the disloyalty of the Supreme Court, the equality of the flashy schools that had been constructed for Negroes in their home towns lately, even Scriptural admonitions against mixing with the hewers of wood. Although some of the carefully nurtured prejudices seemed sincere, the opinions themselves were not as strong as the compulsion to make them appear so for my benefit and each other's. The Ritual, which is gradually dying out among adults in Georgia, appeared to be in full bloom in the younger generation. Still, one involuntary sign of progress kept creeping out. Most of the clichés followed a clause such as "We may not be able to do anything about it, and I'm sure not going to risk my butt trying, but . . ." or "All right, they have a legal right to be here, but . . ." Nobody in the Sigma Nu house had been granting that right in 1961. Although the admission made the clichés sound even feebler, it confirmed Dean Tate's theory that the boys who thought they could do something about clearing the campus of Negroes were gone. One Sigma Nu actually offered the opinion that if Hamilton Holmes did better on the college boards than he did, Hamilton Holmes deserved to be admitted to Georgia before he was. The speaker was slightly drunk, and his fraternity brothers, having booed him, assured me that he didn't realize what he was saying.

About the only cliché that the Sigma Nus forgot—that "you can't legislate morality"—has often been cited by those who maintain that a traditional system of segregation cannot be ended by a court order. In fact, in the South since 1954 the pattern has been exactly the opposite, and the University of Georgia turned out to be no exception. Even the self-conscious chorus of Sigma Nus accepted the right of Charlayne and Hamilton to attend the university—a right that did not, of course, depend on their acceptance. Most of the students had apparently got used to seeing Charlayne and Hamilton on the campus, without caring much one way or the other, just as most people in Atlanta, Savannah, and Macon had got used to seeing Negroes ride in the front of formerly segregated buses and use formerly all-white libraries and lunch counters. Some students at Georgia—the members of Charlayne's summer session classics course, for example, who were suddenly confronted with a more than equal Negro—were forced to change some of their views by the fact of integration. And a few, at first wanting an open university more than they wanted segregation, then appalled by the riot staged in the name of segregation, then feeling a certain amount of natural sympathy for people in a lonely spot, eventually went beyond the view that Charlayne and Hamilton were at Georgia because of some narrow and unfortunate legal right, and began to believe that they should be there.

Some of the students in the last category were members of the Westminster Disciplined Study Community, a group of about a dozen undergraduates, including Harold Black, who met at Westminster House every weekday morning at seven-fifteen to discuss religion and related subjects. About the only member of the group who was also influential in the Greek establishment was Winston Stephens, a former president of the Women's Student Government Association, a member of Kappa Alpha Theta, and the daughter of Robert Stephens, who represents Athens and the surrounding area in Congress. Winston, a tall, thin, thoughtful girl, was also in Charlayne's honors seminar, and after the class one day I arranged to meet her for a talk about how the white students had reacted to integration.

She agreed with Tommy Johnson on the attitude of

most students. "People don't notice as much if they see Charlayne or Hamilton on the campus," she said. "But they'll remark on it if they have a class with them, especially if they think it will mean some physical contact. One of my sorority sisters has a physical-education class in folk dancing with one of the Negro freshmen, and she's quite upset about it. I don't think the attitude has changed in respect to integration. Most people feel they're here, and nothing can be done. There's no pressure against being normally friendly. I always say hello to Charlayne. I sat down in the library to study with her the other night and nobody said anything. We're in that seminar together now, so I'll probably be seeing her more. Sometimes, when something happens—like when I heard at Westminster this week about a boy who was threatened because he ate with the two freshmen—I'm so shocked, because I get so I think that kind of thing is over."

I asked Winston what the reaction would be if she had lunch with Charlayne.

"It would depend on who saw it," she said. "A sorority sister of mine, who was head of Women's Student Government when Charlayne came, was asked to escort her to one or two places—as part of her official duties—and she got a lot of criticism. The sorority members feel that what one member does reflects on the whole sorority. Even if people don't remember the girl's name, they can usually identify the group. I'm afraid we classify by groups here."

I got the impression that whereas Tommy Johnson hadn't considered the idea of having lunch with Hamilton, Winston would have lunch with Charlayne if she felt like it, and I was curious how she managed to maintain her connection with the slightly suspect Westminster group, which, after all, included a Negro, and still pre-

serve her standing in a society so conscious of the group
that the deviation of one sorority member casts a stigma
on the whole sorority.

"It doesn't come up too often," Winston said. "I avoid
talking about it. People know I go there, but nobody says
much. I suppose I'm not ready to make a public declara-
tion about it all. It's a personal thing. I think I don't say
much about it because of my family, but maybe that's an
excuse. I feel good sometimes that Charlayne and Hamilton are here. Everybody raised in the South has to go
through a time of getting used to the change in status,
and I think the earlier in your life you do it the better off
you are."

White students who did want to see Charlayne and
Hamilton socially were handicapped by limited entertainment facilities in Athens, for, even though Athens is
one of the most progressive small cities in Georgia, the
court order desegregating the university naturally did
not desegregate the town. In the South, the normal
Chamber of Commerce method of nicknaming a city is
to claim that it is the Southern version of some other
city, so Atlanta is the New York of the South, Birmingham is the Pittsburgh of the South, New Orleans is the
Paris of the South, and Nashville—which has a neo-
Greek state capitol, an exact replica of the Parthenon not
far away, and a university that is occasionally called the
Princeton of the South—is the Athens of the South. Since
this method might have left Athens, which actually *is* the
Athens of the South, with a redundant title, headline
writers in Georgia long ago settled on "the Classic City"
as a sobriquet. But there is little about Athens that is
classic, whether the term is taken to apply to ancient
Greece or the Old South. The town does not have the

traditional town square built around a county courthouse and a Confederate monument. It does have some
beautiful ante-bellum houses, a sprinkling of commemo-
rative plaques, and a pleasant history that has always
been intermingled with that of the university it was
founded to house. Athens, which has a population of
about forty thousand, has never been a mill town, and its
leaders, who often, through family ties if not actual em-
ployment, consider themselves "university people," have,
compared to those in other Georgia towns, usually led
wisely. The atmosphere became more cosmopolitan after
the Second World War, when three or four northern
firms established plants nearby, one of them, a Westing-
house factory, moving in seventy-five families—execu-
tives and technical people—from Pennsylvania. In 1959,
Athens acquired one of the state's first active chapters of
HOPE (Help Our Public Education), which worked to
keep schools open long before that effort was made almost respectable by the report of the Sibley Commission.
One of its organizers, a former city attorney and part-
time Georgia professor, whose ancestors include a president and a chancellor of the university, was later elected
Superior Court judge for the area. Clarke County, which
is almost entirely Athens, has always had one of the most
liberal voting records in the state. (In fact, the men who
control Athens tend to be more enlightened politically
than the men who control the university. The University
System Board of Regents is composed of one member
from each of Georgia's ten congressional districts and five
members from the state at large, all appointed, for stag-
gered terms, by the governor. The best known regent is
Roy Harris, who for years has been Georgia's most vocal
racist and who was formerly a political power in the state.
Although Harris was discredited throughout most of Geor-

gia even before he made an abusive phone call to President Aderhold the night Charlayne and Hamilton were admitted to the university, he is probably more at home at a meeting of the Board of Regents than he would be in any Athens board room. In the 1962 primary campaign, when Carl Sanders made his bid for the gubernatorial nomination by promising "a new era in Georgia"—he was nominated overwhelmingly—eight of the fifteen regents appeared on the platform at the opening campaign rally for Marvin Griffin, a former governor, whose administration probably set state records for racism and venality. When the Atlanta *Constitution* criticized the supposedly nonpolitical regents for backing Griffin, their chairman— then Robert O. Arnold, a man who swore during the Athens trial that all he knew about the fund cut-off law was what he read in the papers—asserted that several other regents were also for Griffin but had been unable to be at the rally.)

During the time Charlayne and Hamilton were at Georgia, the white leaders of Athens, working with the Negro community, quietly integrated the town's department-store lunch counters and its bus station, and, I gathered, from what people in Athens said, that the only reason more progress had not been made was that the city lacked a tough and effective Negro leadership to apply the pressure.

Even before any move was made in the direction of desegregation, the attitude of the white community in Athens toward nonwhites had been softened by the presence of foreign students at the university. They had begun coming thirty or forty years earlier, and when Charlayne and Hamilton started their senior year, one hundred and sixteen foreign students, from thirty-seven countries, were enrolled at Georgia. The largest lot— nineteen—was from Cambodia, which has an exchange program with the Agriculture School whereby Cambodian students attend Georgia and Georgia professors teach in Cambodia. The second largest—eleven—was from Syria, the Ford Foundation having established grants for Syrians who wished to study agriculture and rural education in Georgia, since Georgia is very similar to Syria in climate, geography, and soil, not to speak of politics. The university also had four students from India, three from the Philippines, and one or two apiece from Pakistan, Thailand, most of the countries in Europe and South America, and practically everywhere else except black Africa. Foreign students are carefully looked after by the university, which makes a conscious attempt, sometimes successful and sometimes not, to integrate them into normal student life.

As long as the dark-skinned students wear their native costumes, they can count on the hospitality of Athens. I had heard that Indian girls were advised to abandon any thought of switching from saris to American dress, but when I visited the foreign students' office at Georgia the assistant director said, "We usually don't have to tell them; they get the word." There was an uncomfortable situation several years ago when a particularly dark Sikh, moved equally by a natural desire to dress like his fellows and by the difficulty of getting turbans laundered in Athens, Georgia, declared a few weeks after he arrived that he was going to cut his hair and give up his turban. Concerned lest the Sikh be taken for an American, the foreign students' office prevailed upon another foreign student to remind him of how disappointed his father might be if the old traditions were flouted, and the Sikh decided to postpone his haircut. He finally did give up his turban the following fall, but by then he was known in Athens and everything worked out all right.

There have been few incidents involving the foreign

students, but, despite their presence and the generally progressive record of the town, many places are not open to Negroes. Unless they put on a turban or a sari—something that Negroes in the South have done occasionally—the Negro students at Georgia could go to no movie theaters except the one for Negroes, the Harlem Theatre, and to no restaurants and no beer parlors. Hamilton went to the movies at the Harlem Theatre occasionally, but Charlayne and Mary Frances Early quickly decided that it was no place for girls. "We went once, but never again," Charlayne said. "They were screaming and yelling, and it was a filthy place. A cat and her kittens were wandering around in there. I wouldn't be surprised if the kittens were born there."

Because the university is legally desegregated and the town is not, Charlayne and the girls could go to the snack bar in the basement of their dormitory but not to the lunch counter on the ground floor of an apartment building right across the street. When Charlayne and Hamilton went to a football game, they sat in the senior section, while the Negroes from Athens sat segregated in a narrow band of seats called "the crow's nest." Still, Athens had not been totally unaffected by the presence of Negroes at the university. For one of her journalism courses, Charlayne observed the local magistrate's court for a week, sitting with a white boy in the courtroom, and she was treated with friendliness. She also ate occasionally at Woolworth's with white students after the desegregation of the lunch counter there. All the Negro students at Georgia made a point of using the main waiting room at the bus station. And the First Presbyterian Church, on many Sundays during the school year, included in its distinguished and conservative congregation of university faculty and Athens business leaders Harold Black, a Negro Baptist from Atlanta.

10

Harold Black had originally gone to the First Presbyterian Church with some of his friends after a Sunday-morning Bible class at Westminster House, where he was a regular participant in its Disciplined Study Community morning meetings, its Wednesday-night seminars, its Sunday-evening supper programs, and just about anything else that was going on. In the first months of the university's integration, Westminster House had been the headquarters for the Students for Constructive Action and the scene of a lot of discussion about race relations, and Corky King, its minister during the first year and a half Charlayne and Hamilton were at Georgia, had on occasion become personally involved in the integration —accompanying Mary Frances Early to the dining hall after somebody had thrown a lemon at her, having Hamilton to dinner every Tuesday when he became dejected during his second spring at Georgia. On my second visit, I found that the Westminster House seminars and study groups still provided about the only outlet for students who wanted to go deeper than fraternity-house conversations, and that Westminster was still the only place where a Negro was accepted without question.

Westminster House is a big red-brick building not far up the street from Center Myers and the Continuing Education Center. The first time I went there looking for Harold Black—I failed to find him, either in any of the seminar rooms or in the bright, spacious living room—I had a talk with its minister, the Reverend Roland Perdue, in order to find out how a Presbyterian society had happened to become the center of dissent at Georgia. Perdue is a friendly, muscular Atlantan who was an all-Atlantic Coast Conference tackle in 1954, when he captained the University of North Carolina football team. He said that Westminster had acquired its unusual role on campus mainly through his predecessors. The pastor who preceded Corky King was an outspoken liberal, and King was so active that in 1962, when he was encouraged to leave by the board—consisting of thirteen Athens and university Presbyterians—that watches over Westminster House, he was generally considered to be the only job casualty of Georgia's integration. But the board had hired King knowing perfectly well that he was just about as outspoken as his predecessor, and, instead of finding a champion of caution to replace him, it had hired Perdue, who, when they asked him, said he did not believe in segregation. An influential Presbyterian in Athens later told me that the board, which was not entirely above suspicion itself among conservative Presbyterians, had no real objection to King's opinions but preferred a pastor who, unlike King, had had some experience with a congregation as well as with students and who tended to start at theology and end up at social problems rather than working the other way around. Also, my informant acknowledged, the board might have thought that Perdue was a bit more moderate than he was.

Perdue could be called a moderate if so many Southern businessmen, editors, and ministers had not used the word to mean not taking any stand at all. Although he believed that segregation was wrong, he had come to Georgia, he told me, as pastor to all the students rather than as a crusader, and he had not sought out Harold Black. But when Harold sought out Westminster, he was accepted as an unquestioned part of the group and became a good friend of Perdue. The Georgia Westminster House had declined to attend a state conference of college Presbyterian groups held in segregated facilities in Covington, but, as Perdue had pointed out in a letter to the conference director, "*not* because the place is segregated but because we can not *all* freely go as a group." The distinction, Perdue thought, was important for a group that had gone beyond talking about Negroes to include one. "I think Harold is a lot less nervous than he was," Perdue said. "It's kind of a dead issue here. We often forget he's a Negro, and only realize it when we want to go to the theater as part of the program, and realize we can't. I hope the time will come, of course, when Harold won't need Westminster as much as he needs it now. But until it does, we're here for the students. We don't have a sign out saying, 'Everybody welcome, especially Negroes.' But everybody *is* welcome."

It seemed obvious that if Corky King and his predecessor had not talked sympathetically about Negroes, none of the students frequenting Westminster House would have been likely to bring one along with him. But now, thanks to the two earlier pastors and Perdue, Westminster appeared to be the one place at Georgia that had gone from conscious acceptance to near normality—to the point where it seemed almost natural for Harold to go with the other students to the First Presbyterian Church one Sunday after Bible class. It may have seemed almost natural to the students at Westminster House, that is. To the congregation of the First Presbyterian Church, the oldest church in Athens, it could not have seemed natural at all. At Perdue's suggestion I went to see the minister there, the Reverend William Adams, to find out how his congregation had reacted.

The First Presbyterian Church, which is known in Athens as First Church, was founded by Moses Waddell, an early non-Yale president of the university, in 1820. It is an impressive granite fortress on Hancock Avenue, next door to the Federal Building where some of its members —among them Walter Danner, who is an elder as well as a registrar—had testified in the trial to desegregate the university. I met Adams, a young man from South Carolina, in his office late that afternoon. He told me that during the brief wave of kneel-ins two or three years before, many white churches in the South had decided what their policy would be if Negroes came to pray with them. The Session, or board of elders, of First Church had decided that all visitors would be seated as space allowed, and the policy had been reaffirmed the previous autumn when Harold Black began to go to Westminster House and the possibility of his attending First Church occurred to Adams.

"We haven't checked on this, but I think we're the first church in the deep South to have a Negro worship with whites on a continuing basis," Adams said. "It's strange.

The people thought it would come one Sunday with no warning, when a Cadillac with New York license plates would roll up and eight people would get out and say, 'We demand that you seat us.' They were relieved when it didn't happen that way, but now they say, 'Why couldn't we have had a kneel-in and had it over with?' Nobody got up and left conspicuously the first day, though some people in the back may have. We did have that happen with one family the second time he came. Some people don't come on the Sundays he's here. We have had people get as far as the vestibule and realize he was here and turn away. I don't think any remarks have been made to him. The real antagonism has been toward the students who brought him—some of them sons of our members. People used to complain that the students didn't come to church, and wonder how we could attract them. Now they're complaining that the students take all the seats. There was a lot of pressure to change the policy. Some people wanted to set aside a special place for him. But the policy was there and the Session has stuck by it. We've avoided a congregational meeting so far, and our attendance is about the same. What will happen during the building-fund campaign we've just started for a church addition I don't know. I get the normal abusive letters and phone calls. Or I suppose it's normal—I'll never look at it that way." He showed me an unsigned letter about the perils of intermarriage; it was written on the program of the previous Sunday's service. It surprised me that some members of First Church—all of whom appeared relatively enlightened, well brought up and publicly Christian—should be so strongly opposed to a Negro's attending services that they would write abusive letters to their own minister. "A majority of the people have accepted it but are not happy about it," said Adams. "Only a

small percentage of the people believe that this is good
or right. I'm only the eighth minister First Church has
had, in a hundred and forty-three years. It wouldn't be
easy to bring *any* strange element into this church. The
people here tend to think in terms of what's coming next.
Who else will come? Will there be a Negro member? Each
step will present more complications. I did think they
were making an adjustment, but last Sunday, when Harold sat next to a white girl from Westminster for the first
time, it all started up again. By and large, though, I'm
proud of our church and proud of our people. Even those
who have argued in the Session against letting Harold
come here have done so on the basis that it will hurt the
church—that we'll lose donations, for instance. It's an argument among people whose first concern is for the
church. Of course, the whole *purpose* of the church is to
get people to come. But this thing is something we haven't
looked for. We've been caught, and it hasn't been easy.
Still, everybody in the South is going to get caught
sooner or later, and maybe they'll be able to see from our
experience that things can be worked out."

The other Negro students I had talked with disagreed
about just how much trouble Harold Black was having
as the first Negro in a men's dormitory, but they were
unanimous in declaring that he would be the last one to
admit that anything was bothering him. "That Harold is
some boy," I was told by Mattie Jo Arnold, the Negro
graduate student in the Music Department, who often
gave him a ride back to Atlanta on week ends. "He and
Charlayne are more forward than the rest of us. Charlayne has formed her own friends on campus; they eat
together and study together. And so has Harold. I think
it's a matter of personality. And I think it's fine. Somebody

should go there and show them—well, that we're okay. But that Harold has his own ways, there's no doubt about that. One thing, when somebody is giving him trouble, Harold will wait until the guy is with some of his own crowd and then give him a big hello. It just embarrasses the guy to pieces. I used to think Harold was conceited— well, he is—but now that I've got to know him, I think he's real swinging."

I finally caught up with Harold Black, and, as everybody had predicted, it was at Westminster House, where he was studying. He turned out to be a tall, thin boy with very thick hair and a mustache. Roland Perdue lent us his office to talk in, and I asked Harold why he had insisted on living in the dormitory and which of the many accounts of his life there was accurate.

"I had to find out for myself," he said. "I figured I could always move out, but it would be hard to move in. I didn't want to have any regrets. I'm real pleased with it. Hamp's said a number of times he's lonely for friends. I'm not lonely for friends. Plenty of times, people ask me, 'Is Hamilton Holmes still at Georgia?' Not one of my friends has ever seen him. You can't find people who're going to go clear over to his neighborhood and say, 'Come over to the room.' Hamilton and I are different people, and I have a lot of respect for him, but I have to do this my own way. Of course, Hamp probably couldn't have done it my way, being the first, but the dorm is the best thing that's happened to me in this university. I came to *this* place with one of my friends from the dorm. I've met every one of my best friends in the dorm. We sit around each other's room and play chess and bridge—I'm teaching them another game, bid-whist—and sometimes they say, 'Hey, Harold, let's go down to the Old South for a couple of beers,' or, 'Hey, Harold, let's go to the movies.' We have some jokes, but you know they're your friends because they meet some opposition for knowing you, so they have to be your friends. These are my friends. I know them and I trust them, and they trust me. The main thing about the girls is that they're isolated in a room all by themselves. Down there, they might as well be living off campus. If they put them up there with the rest of the girls, things would be different. They might get a little opposition from some of the girls, but they would make friends, too."

Harold smiled when he talked about "opposition"—his word for the harassment he had had to put up with in the dormitory. He seemed to treat the trouble as a game between pals trying to outwit each other, and seemed to enjoy telling the stories, often ending them on a humorous note. "There are pranks," he admitted. "I won't deny that. For instance, they put chewing gum in my lock. But now I'm prepared." He pulled a nail file and an eye dropper out of his pocket. "I always carry these. One or the other will take care of anything they put in there. I either dig it out with the file or melt it with hot water. So it takes me another thirty seconds to get in my room—I don't mind. We had a little trouble with the vent. They used to drop firecrackers through it. Of course, I'm a very heavy sleeper, and sometimes I didn't even wake up; I moved my bed away from the door right away. Once, they strapped a cherry bomb to the vent and blew it out completely. The proctor came and woke me up, and I asked him what was the matter. He said, 'The vent,' and I said, 'What vent?' He said that was the point. But really, it wasn't that bad. I figured what could they think of next. And they thought of a few things. They were pretty ingenious. One day, my room was almost flooded; they had put a balloon full of water through the vent." As he

talked, Harold seemed to find flooding even more entertaining than the cherry bomb. "I thought all that stuff was
funny," he went on. "And it wasn't only me. Like, I had
three windows broken out, but the first one was in the
winter quarter, not the fall, and a proctor down the hall
had every window broken. If somebody upstairs had a
window broken, I didn't think they were probably aiming
for mine and missed. Nobody could miss one of those big
windows. They used to write on the door, but usually the
janitor would wipe it off before I saw it, or one of my
friends would wipe it off. We did have some trouble with
that vent. Somebody scratched 'Nigger Nest' on it. But,
you know, I'm glad they did. This way, it's there, and after
the first couple of days nobody even noticed it any more.
It's better than worrying every time if something is there.
The dorm's okay. The only thing is—the next Negro boy
in there, they ought to give him a roommate. He ought to
have somebody in there to talk to.

    "I don't get much opposition on the campus. I eat at
Memorial Hall, and they look up and look back down. Tonight, when I went in with my brother Charles, who's
visiting me from Purdue, they kept looking. They
thought, 'My God, he's got a roommate!' Plenty of times,
when I'm with my friends, if somebody says something,
we'll go over there and see what they want. Plenty of
times, I'll say something back. I don't believe in turning
the other cheek. I've been to two pep rallies. I went to
the intersquad game. I went to the freshman football
game—at night. I cheered for our team. I didn't stand up
when they played 'Dixie,' of course. I got a little opposition
for that, but most people thought it was funny. I play
clarinet in the Air Force R.O.T.C. band, and if I join the
Dixie Red Coats, the school band, I'll have to play 'Dixie.'
I don't care; let them have their fun. Once, Mattie Jo

Arnold said, 'That's good. You're taking one more step.'
But I can't swallow that. What I'm doing is just floating
along naturally with my friends. Now the church, that
was a step—and the first couple of times after Sunday
school here when they asked me to go, I said to myself,
'No, Harold, that's off campus. They might think you're
crusading.' But finally I decided my friends wanted me to
go and I wanted to go, so we went. But I don't consider
the rest of this a step."

Harold, like Charlayne, disliked admitting that anything he did at Georgia, including his decision to come
in the first place, had any connection with the Cause. He
said, at one point, "Maybe being brought up with the
thought, 'We pay taxes, too, and we can't go down there
and that's not right' might have had some influence." But
he preferred to talk about academic challenge and financial advantages. Like all the other Negro students, he particularly resented the belief, held by so many of the people around him, that he was at Georgia as somebody else's
tool, incapable of making up his own mind about where
he wanted to go to college.

"A lot of the attention is gone," Harold said. "You're the
first person who has ever interviewed me. People in Atlanta, boys I went to high school with, still ask me where
I'm going to school. My preacher in Atlanta, Sam Williams, was president of the N.A.A.C.P. branch last year,
and one Sunday this fall he said, 'Well, haven't you gone
to college yet, Harold?' And I said I was going the next
week. He said, 'Where are you going?' I told him the University of Georgia, and he almost fell over."

One afternoon I arranged to have a talk with "the
girls," Kerry Rushin and Alice Henderson, and when we
met, I was impressed, as I had been before, at how small

they were. They both looked too young to be involved in anything like being among the first Negroes at the University of Georgia—too young, really, even to be in college. We met at the Continuing Education Center, and, suddenly finding myself in what must have been a familiar situation to them, I suggested that we seek the sanctuary of Westminster House, the one place on campus where I knew we would not be stared at as we talked.

Alice had occasionally attended a Sunday-evening program there with Harold Black, but it was Kerry's first visit to Westminster. From having heard them nearly always spoken of together, and watching them break into each other's sentences to finish relating a common experience, I thought of them at first as looking alike. Then I saw that Kerry had a round face and a cheery look, while Alice, who was light-skinned and very thin, had a long, sad face, which always seemed to reflect thoughts of some vague misfortune. They explained to me that much of their isolation had to do with the lack of a base. Harold had his dormitory; Charlayne was in a small school, where people had a chance to get used to her. But both Kerry and Alice, who, like Harold, had been outstanding students in their high schools in Atlanta, were planning to major in zoology, and they wandered in and out of the same large, impersonal classes that Hamilton did, returning to the dormitory—or, occasionally, to the library—to study, and eating at the dining hall either alone or with each other. They were not close to Charlayne, although they shared the same suite; she had little more in common with them than with any other freshmen. All in all, they seemed the most isolated of the Negro students. In some ways, they were treated more naturally than the first students, but what little improvement they had noticed in their reception by other students was, they believed, not lasting. "What we went through, the next Negroes who come will have to go through the same thing," Alice said.

Since the number of invidious remarks directed at the Negro students on the campus was in almost precisely inverse proportion to the students' size, Kerry and Alice heard the most.

"A lot of times, people make remarks in the dining-hall lines," Alice said. "Like, 'I thought I smelled something,' or 'I'm not standing in front of a nigger.' "

"There's a difference between us in how much we hear," Kerry interjected, smiling. "Alice hears some things that I don't."

"There's, say, five a day I hear," Alice said. "Sometimes I don't hear them, but a lot of times it's pretty obvious."

I asked if they thought the situation would always remain the same.

"Until one of us makes an attempt to enter some social activity, it will be the same," Alice said. "Take Harold, for instance. He's in the R.O.T.C. and the R.O.T.C. band. It's a small step, but it's a step. It's up to us to try to enter everything that we have an opportunity to enter, and that we want to do. You come back in a couple of years. Everything won't be perfect, but we'll have integrated more activities, Harold and us. I think we have to. If we didn't, there wouldn't be any use in our being here, the way I look at it."

11

ALICE's willingness to make an estimate of what had to be done was not characteristic. Harold and the girls, eager to be accepted as normal students, usually avoided talking about having a mission at Georgia. But Charlayne and Hamilton, the Student Heroes, had been expected to do a certain amount of talking about it in public from the start. Their attitudes toward public speaking had gradually shifted. As Hamilton became more willing to give up his textbooks and his week-end basketball occasionally for speaking engagements, Charlayne became less interested in speaking at all. During their last few months at Georgia, Hamilton spoke fairly often, usually before church groups around the state or at meetings of his fraternity. After his speech at the Annual Youth Day of Emmanuel Baptist Church, he said, "I tell you how I feel about it. Three years ago, if I got up to say something, it was just a young boy talking. Now we have some respect; people listen because of the situation here. I figure now we can do our people some good. I don't mean go around advocating taking over everything. I'm no radical. But like that speech I made Sunday about going after education."

As one of the outstanding students at Georgia, Hamilton was in a good position to encourage other Negroes to go there and to other white schools as a matter of self-improvement. The University of Georgia may not be a distinguished university, but it seems that way to anybody who has ever seen the three state colleges for Negroes. In fact, after Hamilton's speech at the Phyllis Wheatley Branch of the Y.W.C.A., it occurred to me that he was in the extraordinarily fortunate position of having personal goals that both served and were served by the Cause. Hamilton told the Wheatley audience that the two-and-a-half-year ordeal at Georgia had been worthwhile, because without it he would probably have been unable to get into Emory Medical School. He apparently meant exactly that; the best medical education in the state was his goal, and if he had not gone to Georgia his acceptance by Emory would have been very unlikely. But it was also true that if he, or somebody like him, had not gone to Georgia, the acceptance of *any* Negro by Emory would have been very unlikely. In that sense, Hamilton was, as Charlayne had told me at the beginning of my visit, a more consistent study than she was. He was a Student Hero who was, in his specific collegiate achievements (apart from his willingness to attend Georgia in the first place), a hero. He had satisfied himself and his family and the Cause, even if he was sick of the whole business and was just waiting for the first of June.

During most of the time Charlayne and Hamilton were

at Georgia, Charlayne, outgoing, articulate, and seemingly comfortable in any surroundings, did most of the speaking for both of them. She was much better known than Hamilton, and, unlike Hamilton, who looked forward to week ends in Atlanta, she didn't mind traveling around on week ends. She flew to New York several times to speak before such groups as the N.A.A.C.P. and the Catholic Interracial Council. She went to Pittsburgh for another Catholic Interracial Council conference and to Boston for an N.A.A.C.P. meeting. She participated in a meeting at Skidmore College, in a civil-rights program sponsored by the Methodist Church in Washington, in a Fellowship of Southern Churchmen conference in Nashville. She received an award from the Association of Negro Business and Professional Women at its state convention in Macon, and one from a Negro fraternity at Wayne in Detroit.

But, more and more, Charlayne had come to recognize the irony of spending a week end in New York, where everybody found her charming, and then returning to the long weeks in Athens, where she was likely to be sneered at when she went to the Co-op for a cup of coffee. There was a special kind of loneliness, she discovered, in being the best-known student on campus and a social undesirable at the same time. Moreover, her ambitions were not as easily related to the Cause as Hamilton's—she had no desire to be the Number 1 student at Georgia or to be admitted to Emory Medical School—and she felt a certain hollowness in being honored as a Student Hero without having done anything that was, by the ordinary standards of collegiate success, heroic. Once, discussing a professor who had "made a big thing" out of his role in the integration crisis, Charlayne said, "I just don't think it should be the biggest thing in his life. He's sixty years old. If my experiences here were all I could talk about, I would get really worried. I'd just be a record player. I'm too young to have already done the most important thing in my life. Look, it may be the most exciting or dramatic thing I'll ever do, but I can't think that it's all I'll ever talk about. It doesn't *take* anything. It doesn't take brains, or anything. It just can't be the biggest thing in my life. When I go to those meetings, people try to make me feel that I'm representing the whole Negro race, and that's not right. I'm not representing anybody. I'm not an ideal girl or the perfect student. I don't want to be an ideal girl—just a girl." And what would the ideal be, Charlayne wondered. What was it she was being honored for? What connection did the honors have with the number of friends she had or the number of professors who thought she was bright or the number of young men who thought she was pretty? In addition, Charlayne, as it happened, was of the age and turn of mind to greet any grandiloquent cliché with a shudder—a characteristic that would have made her uncomfortable on any banquet circuit. She had the disquieting habit of juxtaposing an idealistic generalization and one of her own specific experiences. What did "the fight for full emancipation" have to do with driving around Athens because there was no place to stop, or waiting in the *Red and Black* office while everybody else was asked to do something? If everybody was so interested in "the cause of freedom," why didn't anybody do anything about encouraging more Negro high-school seniors to go to Georgia? And why did she have to scratch around before every quarter to get enough money to go back to school?

Early in my return visit to Georgia, I had a chance to accompany Charlayne on one of her last speaking engagements—or, more accurately, one of her last public appearances. She warned me ahead of time that she would have little to say. The occasion was the Freedom Awards Dinner of the N.A.A.C.P. Southeastern Regional Conference, in Tampa. According to the original plans, Charlayne, Hamilton, James Meredith, and Harvey Gantt were all supposed to receive plaques at the dinner. But Hamilton was unable to go, having already promised his fraternity he would give a speech in Cincinnati, and by the time the week of the dinner arrived, Harvey Gantt had also sent word that he would not be able to make it because he was in the middle of exams at Clemson. Charlayne herself was not eager to go, although her father and her grandfather live in Tampa. "I feel like a hypocrite giving those speeches," she told me, "all that We Shall Overcome business. I believe in it, sure. But there are some things I believe that I just don't believe in talking about. And I have to break away from that image business sooner or later. I can't spend my life being an image."

But Charlayne decided she would be an image for one more evening at least, mainly because she had promised Vernon Jordan, then the Georgia field secretary for the N.A.A.C.P., that she would be there. Jordan was a good friend of Charlayne's. Before joining the N.A.A.C.P. staff, he had worked in the office of Donald Hollowell, and had helped plow through the admission records of the university in preparation for the Athens trial.

James Meredith, too, was definitely attending the dinner. I had met him almost exactly two years before, in Jackson, when Mrs. Motley was in Mississippi to file the first motion in the case to get him admitted to the University of Mississippi. At the time, he seemed to me to be about what it would take to battle the Mississippi monolith. Before returning to Georgia, I said something of the

sort to Mrs. Motley, and she agreed. "In Harlem, they
would say Charlayne and Hamilton are 'white,'" she told
me. "In other words, they don't have any of the dis-
advantages of a sharecropper background. But Meredith
is very bitter, a real crusader. He wants to get back at society." While Charlayne and Hamilton were interested
only in getting something approaching a normal education, Mrs. Motley said, Meredith was consciously out to
start the breakdown of the system that had oppressed
him so long, whatever the cost to him. Already twenty-
seven when he applied for admission to Ole Miss, he had
to slow down his courses at Jackson State to avoid earning
his degree before he was accepted. In the simplest terms,
Meredith differed from Charlayne and Hamilton as rural
Mississippi differed from middle-class Atlanta, and some
people who knew all the Student Heroes believed that
even if a middle-class Negro community had existed in
Mississippi, Ole Miss would have had to be left to Meredith. "Meredith is real angry," one of them told me in Atlanta. "He's fighting the battle all the time—everything he
says, everything he does. I'm not sure that Charlayne or
Hamp could have stayed over there as long as he has."

Before the flight to Tampa, while Charlayne and I
were having a drink at the Atlanta airport (it was built
in 1961, with all facilities desegregated), I asked her if
she knew Meredith.

"You mean 'I, James H. Meredith'?" she asked. Charlayne, it turned out, always called Meredith by his full
name, sometimes even including the personal pronoun,
in reference to the rather self-conscious press conferences he had held at Ole Miss. "He called me after the
first few days there," she said. "I had sent him a telegram
wishing him luck, and all that. At first, I didn't believe it
was him when he called. It was kind of awkward, because

we didn't know what to say. I finally asked how things
were going, and he said, 'Listen,' and I could hear the
firecrackers. Then he came through Atlanta last Christmas; he and Hamp's family and Hollowell and a couple of
people came over to the house one night. He's very de-
fensive. We sure weren't trying to trap him, but he never
let down his guard. But James H. Meredith is okay. Of
course, he has about as much sense of humor as Martin
Luther King."

It was hot and sticky in Tampa. Vernon Jordan had
driven to the airport to pick us up, and Charlayne greeted
him by saying, "Only for you, buddy, only for you." Jordan
laughed and packed us into the car for a ride over the
causeway to St. Petersburg, where he had to pick up the
plaques that Charlayne and the others were going to
receive that night. We drove from St. Petersburg to a
Tampa church, where the business part of the conference was in progress, and Charlayne and I waited in the
car while Jordan went in to look for her father. The dinner was to be held in the gymnasium of the Howard W.
Blake Vocational School, a Negro high school in West
Tampa, and Charlayne remarked, "I'm glad it's not at a
church tonight. Meetings in churches always get too
much like mass meetings. Like the meeting they had for
Emancipation Day in Atlanta. Nobody *ever* put on a dis-
play like that. They took the collection twice. First, they
had all those thirty thousand people file up and put in a
contribution, and then the chairman said, 'We know
some of you are just too tired to walk up here,' and passed
around the basket. It started at eleven, and at three it
still wasn't over. I mean, it makes you rather not be eman-
cipated."

Charlayne's father was not at the church, nor was he
at his house, where we drove next. By the time we had

started back through downtown Tampa toward Charlayne's quarters for the night, conversation had languished, despite the efforts of the ebullient Jordan.

Since hotel accommodations for Negroes in Tampa were practically nonexistent, most of the visitors to the convention had been assigned to private houses. Being an important visitor, Charlayne, who had decided not to stay with her father and grandfather, drew what was considered to be the best private house of all, that of Leon Claxon, who, as manager of a dance troupe known as Harlem in Havana, toured the fair circuit for six months a year and lived in a large, Florida-style, pink-brick house the other six.

James Meredith, who was also staying with the Claxons, arrived shortly before the dinner was scheduled to start. Meredith, smiling and friendly, exchanged hearty greetings with Charlayne. He laughed easily, and seemed relieved to be among friends. Jordan told me that this was one of the first trips Meredith had made unescorted by marshals since he had been at Ole Miss, although, Jordan added, the F.B.I. in Tampa had phoned to check his schedule. Shortly after he arrived, Meredith went into his room to change his clothes, and emerged looking much as he had before, like a small, neat, carefully dressed accountant.

Charlayne, who was in the living room, said, "Why, there's James H. Meredith, looking good."

"I thought nobody would ever say *that*," Meredith replied, and everybody laughed.

When we arrived at the gym, Charlayne's father, a handsome and impressive-looking man in full clerical dress, including a large cross hanging from a heavy chain around his neck, was one of a group of people talking in the corridor outside. Colonel Hunter, who has a sonorous voice and a tendency to use phrases like "the essence of American democracy," immediately began introducing Charlayne around. James Popovich, the speech professor who had taken an interest in all of the first Negro students at Georgia, was also there, having transferred to the University of South Florida, in Tampa, the previous fall.

The gymnasium was a large, plain room, its cinderblock walls painted two shades of green, and it was so jammed with long tables that, once seated, a guest was almost immobile. Charlayne and her father sat at the head table. Popovich and I managed to find two seats at the end of a table toward the back of the room. The dinner guests, some of them delegates to the three-day conference, others Tampa residents, were well dressed and in a convivial mood. Four or five white reporters leaned against one wall, looking uncomfortable. The master of ceremonies turned out to be Charlayne's host, Leon Claxon, a roly-poly man with a quick, state-fair delivery. He began the program immediately after the invocation, and at the same time the waiters began to squeeze up and down the tables serving dinner.

There was no public-address system, and the only person on the program who could be heard clearly through the clatter of silverware and conversation was the first speaker, Mrs. Ruby Hurley, the Southeastern regional director; she had a well-pitched voice and a clarity of diction that brought occasional nods of professional approval from Popovich. Mrs. Hurley began announcing branch contributions to the N.A.A.C.P. Freedom Fund, one of the main sources of the organization's operating expenses. Seventy-five dollars was reported from Jacksonville, a hundred dollars from Savannah, a hundred from Jackson, Mississippi. Mrs. Hurley expressed amazement at the generosity of little Perry, Florida, which presented fifty dollars from the main branch and thirty-five dollars from its youth council. "You know what Perry is like?" she asked the audience. "It's a smaller city like Birmingham. And if you don't know what Birmingham is, it's like any place in Mississippi."

The audience murmured agreement, and I could feel its comfort in being in the crowded but safe gymnasium of the Howard W. Blake Vocational School in West Tampa instead of in Perry or Birmingham or Mississippi.

Claxon took over from Mrs. Hurley to announce that he was the holder of five N.A.A.C.P. life memberships—two, at five hundred dollars apiece, for him and his wife, and three, at one hundred a piece, for his children. He said that a well-known businessman, a leading citizen named Lee, had confessed to him not long ago that he was not a life member, because nobody had ever asked him to be. "He's here tonight," Claxon said, "and I'm asking him to buy three life memberships." Lee stood up and said he would not be high-pressured; he had come intending to buy one life membership, and he would do that. Following two vocal solos—"Temptation" and "September Song" —Aaron Henry, the Mississippi N.A.A.C.P. conference president, presented Meredith with his plaque for "furthering the cause of higher education in Mississippi." By that time, enough people had been served so that we had to lean forward to catch even an occasional phrase of Meredith's speech, which started out with "It is with deep honor and satisfaction" and included, toward the end, "satisfying to see so many young people." The audience gave Meredith a standing ovation, quite a feat in the packed gymnasium. They did not try it again for Charlayne, who received only enthusiastic applause as she accepted her plaque and said, her soft voice even less audible than Meredith's, "You write me, 'We prayed for you.'"

I don't like that past tense. There's still a few months to go. So keep praying. And keep supporting the N.A.A.C.P. This fight is not going to end when Hamp and I graduate from Georgia and Meredith graduates from Mississippi."

Claxon introduced Charlayne's father and grandfather; a plaque was presented to George Allen, the first Negro to graduate from the University of Florida Law School; and then Mrs. Hurley rose again, to present branch awards for gains in membership. Jackson County, Florida, won the award in the under-200-quota category, having come up with 228 members in 1962; Coahoma County, Mississippi, Henry's local branch, won the 200-to-500-quota group, with 419 members; and Macon, which had had 429 members in 1961 and had been asked for 500 in 1962, ended up with 820, to win in the over-500 category. Georgia won the Harry T. Moore award for state membership, and the Florida delegation got a mild chiding from Mrs. Hurley; the award was named for a Florida N.A.A.C.P. executive who was killed in the dynamiting of his house, she pointed out, but Florida had never won it. Since the N.A.A.C.P. is fundamentally a membership organization, what goes on at one of its dinners gives the first impression of being rather far removed from the basic problems of civil rights. The awards, even when they are given to branches that have made some real progress against segregation—in Macon, for instance, the parks and buses had been integrated, largely through the efforts of the local N.A.A.C.P. branch —are given for gains in membership and in fund-raising, with integration mentioned only in passing. It is true that the conference program included seminars on how to get voters registered as well as on how to get members for the local branch, and I knew that for the average Southern Negro merely becoming a member is an important step forward, reflecting a change in his attitude as well as providing financial support for a program that could eventually affect his life; yet it was difficult to escape the feeling during the dinner that the cycle of recruiting members in order to raise money in order to recruit members went on without anyone's ever coming to grips with the issues.

As Mrs. Hurley completed the branch awards, she asked if she had missed any branch donations, and a very small old man shuffled toward the front of the room. Mrs. Hurley, who seemed to know him well, introduced him as R. A. Reddick, who had been secretary of the Live Oak, Florida, branch for twenty years. "And I want to tell you what kind of place Live Oak is," she went on. "That's in Suwannee County, and every time I hear the song 'Swanee River' I think about Live Oak and the time I went to speak there a few years ago. When I got through with my speech, they were driving me back to the airport and they seemed anxious that I get out before nightfall. I asked why, and they told me this story—you correct me if I'm wrong, Mr. Reddick. There was a ten-year-old boy in Live Oak named James Howard. He worked around a store there. One day, in about 1943, the storekeeper's daughter heard him whistling a tune and she asked him to write the words down for her on a piece of paper. Well, the storekeeper saw the piece of paper later, and he took it for a love letter and asked who had written it. The daughter told him it was James Howard. So the storekeeper and some of his friends got this boy—ten years old—and took him down by the Swannee River and tied him up. Then some of them went to get the boy's father and brought him down to the river. Some of them held the father so he could see, and the others took this ten-year-old boy and threw him in the river. That's the kind of place Mr. Reddick lives in."

The audience looked at Reddick in silence. The old man had been nodding during the speech, as if he were recalling James Howard and his father and his neighbors. "Fifteen dollars from the Live Oak branch," Mrs. Hurley said. The audience applauded. As Mrs. Hurley thanked him, Reddick nodded again, and smiled, and shuffled back to his chair.

Next came more music, this time by the Youth Choir of Laurel, Mississippi—about thirty Negro children, of all sizes. Before they started to sing, Mrs. Hurley told of the sacrifices that Dr. B. E. Murph, a Laurel dentist, had made to keep the choir going and get it to a number of regional and national N.A.A.C.P. conventions. She asked for donations to help the singers get back to Laurel and to pay for their dinners.

When the choir sat down, after two spirituals, Meredith stood up to make a surprise comment on the Laurel students. "People always ask me what keeps me going," he said. "Those people keep me going. I've had a choice in everything I've done. But they don't have a choice."

Then Claxon stood up for some more fund-raising. "I don't want to hear about that last five dollars for the choir," he said. "We're talking now about that second five dollars. Who in this row has five dollars for freedom?"

The meeting ended with a strong chorus of "God Be with You Till We Meet Again" and a benediction by Charlayne's grandfather, who is also a minister. Charlayne and Meredith stayed on the dais autographing programs while, at a table below them, Mrs. Hurley and two or three helpers counted up the donations.

From the gym, I went back to Claxon's with Charlayne for a party in his downstairs recreation room, which was lined with pictures of the Harlem in Havana dance troupe. The party got off to a poor start for Popovich, when he told Meredith that his experience at Georgia had

been that the university theater was a good place to begin integrating university events, since the Drama Department was generally cooperative. "It's not a matter of
cooperation," Meredith told him. "I have a student activity card, and I have a right to go." Charlayne and I
were cornered for a while by a man from South Carolina,
who told us that Harvey Gantt was his protégé. Soon, however, the individual conversations broke up, for Claxon
began to tell some jokes. "You know, Ross Barnett said,
'This is the darkest day of my life' when you got into
school there," Claxon said, pointing to Meredith. "But
then some cat next to him said, 'That's not the darkest
day. The darkest day is when you get to Heaven and a
voice says, "Hello dere, Ah am de Lawd." ' " It was an old
joke, but it got a good laugh, especially from Meredith.

    Later, Meredith remarked that the dinner had been too
long. "We're going to have to think of a better way to keep
up enthusiasm and morale," he said. "This is a drawn-out
way." He also said he was sorry that Harvey Gantt and
Hamilton had not been able to attend the meeting. "Did
you see Hamp on TV a couple of months ago?" he asked.
"Hamp's my boy. He said that the time he made them
think he had a gun was the first time he got any respect. He said he hated to do it that way; then he sat back
and said, 'But I had to.' That's my kind of talk. Hamp's
okay."

    After the party, Popovich and I left together, and he
anticipated my first question by assuring me that his de-
parture from the University of Georgia had nothing to
do with his role in its integration. "The administration
could have very easily got word to me to slow down, but
they never did," he said. The members of the Georgia
faculty, Popovich believed, treated all the Negro students
fairly, but, except for the two or three who had invited

Charlayne and Hamilton to dinner, few went out of their way to make them more comfortable. "They espouse integration after a couple of drinks, and then start talking about their mortgages," said Popovich.

"Hamp, more than any other kid in that situation, was really interested in what the university could give him academically," Popovich went on. "But Hamp was also the first one to attend a university event. We had an arena theater, and I arranged the audience so he was surrounded by reasonable people, and I was very careful about the people facing him. Close to a hundred people came up to me after the play, and the funny thing was that more of them mentioned how nice they thought it was that he was there than how they liked the play. Charlayne resented being managed. She wanted to do things her own way."

On the plane back to Atlanta the next morning I asked Charlayne what she thought of James H. Meredith's unexpected speech about the Laurel Youth Choir. I was hoping, I think, for a bit of humor to lighten the journey, and her answer surprised me.

"You know, I almost cried when I heard those kids sing," she said. "Did you hear that first spiritual, 'I've Been 'Buked and I've Been Scorned'? You know, it's written 'buked instead of *re*buked because that's the way it was supposedly sung on the plantation. But I don't think those kids know the difference; they probably think that's the way it's pronounced. I remember, in Covington, when I was a little girl, even though my father had been to college, there were words I mispronounced for years. I'd leave the whole middle syllable out sometimes. And in some of those letters people sent me after the riot a lot of the words were spelled phonetically, with one or two syllables missing. Meredith is right. He's had a choice in everything he did, and those kids haven't. They were just pitiful."

We talked about whether the money and energy spent on the choir might better be spent more directly in Laurel.

Charlayne thought that was possible. "I don't know how many people the choir reaches," she said. "Take last night—those people were convinced anyway."

I said maybe the choir was worthwhile just because it had moved both her and Meredith, who otherwise, as they went from meeting to meeting, might grow as cynical as she sometimes seemed to want me to believe she was.

"No. There's always something or somebody at those meetings that makes me want to cry," she said. "Like that little old man from Live Oak. He didn't want to make a big thing of how much he's done. He just came up there with his fifteen dollars."

12

THE morale of both Charlayne and Hamilton had reached
its low point during the spring of their junior year. "I
guess my mother's right about last spring," Hamilton told
me on my last visit to the campus. "I used to walk by those
frat houses, and the boys would be out there playing ball,
and I'd think, What is there for me to do except go home
and sit? A thousand times I wished I were back at Morehouse. But then I thought, Look, I wouldn't have been going to Emory Medical School, and I wouldn't have been
able to travel around and meet all those people—I like
that kind of thing—and I matured a lot here. I had to ma-
ture or just die out. I might not have gone to medical
school at all if I had stayed at Morehouse. The last semester there, I wasn't doing very well. I was playing football,
and everything, and I got so I just didn't care. I guess I'm
glad I came down here. I might have ended up a bum.

Although I guess not. With my dad and mother right
there, and my granddaddy, I guess I would have shaped
up."

Charlayne insisted that her troubles that spring had
nothing to do with the Issue but were simply the result
of her trying to get her required courses in science and
mathematics out of the way at the same time—an attempt that resulted in Charlayne's being put on academic
probation and having to go to summer school.

"I really *am* inferior when it comes to science and
math," she said. "Those guys are right."

In her two and a half years at Georgia, where even
philosophy tests are usually made up of true-false and
multiple-choice questions, Charlayne's grades fluctuated
wildly; she was eventually graduated with a B average,
but her individual grades ran the gamut from academic
probation to honors. Occasionally, she became really interested in a course, such as the honors seminar in the
art, music, and drama of the twentieth century (Joe
Schwarz, one of the instructors in the course, had helped
her get permission to take it, even though she was not in
the honors program), but ordinarily, I was told by a professor who knew both Hamilton and Charlayne, Hamilton
was not only more likely to remember what he read in the
textbooks but also more likely to be reading them. Charlayne could wander off into a flirtation with Yevtushenko
("I love it; it doesn't seem like poetry"), or end up driving
around Athens. Her initial reaction to the journalism
courses that made up twenty-five per cent of her schedule
was to accept the advice of reporters covering the integration that she consider switching to English. She changed
her mind when two or three professors warned her that
the Georgia English Department still reflected the influence of the Southern Agrarians, a group of Vanderbilt

University English professors and writers who believed for a while in the twenties that everything would be all right in the South if the cultured benevolence they attached to plantation days could just be brought back.

"Some of the professors think the only way I can succeed around here is academic," said Charlayne. "A couple of them liked to have had a heart attack when I went on probation. One of them told me he thought Negroes should be screened carefully, so only the best students would come. I think we ought to have all kinds. Hamp tells me I'm not serious enough, because I don't want to make Phi Beta Kappa. I didn't really have any philosophy when I came about how I would approach it, but sooner or later I figured the only way I could benefit from this was to get personally involved." Personal involvement proved to be a trickier battlefield for Charlayne than the straight academic contest was for Hamilton. She was in the infirmary off and on throughout her stay—mainly with stomach trouble. After two years of weekly arguments with her Atlanta doctor, Clinton Warner, whose wife had attended the graduate schools of both Georgia (as a commuter) and Georgia State, Charlayne finally admitted occasionally that her stomach trouble might be psychosomatic. Dr. Warner, who was one of the original A.C.C.A. group and was the first Negro to buy a house on the other side of Atlanta's wall—but no goody-goody—says that Charlayne would have had a nervous stomach wherever she went to school, but that the additional strain of Georgia almost certainly made it worse.

Charlayne also had problems in Atlanta. Unlike Hamilton, who had never really left the Negro community, she sometimes felt that she was living in limbo. "It's disillusioning that we still have this conscious barrier of color in our own people," she said. "You should see the way they treat any white I bring back to Atlanta." She was further disillusioned to discover that the Atlanta Negro community contained quite a few people who liked to play one of the pioneers off against the other, handing out the plaques and money to whichever of them seemed to be in the lead. Some people were even called "pro-Hamp" or "pro-Charlayne," and being pro one usually meant being anti the other. A Hamilton partisan might point to Hamilton's extraordinary academic performance as the proper goal of the first Negro at Georgia and complain that Charlayne did not meet her responsibilities, or might accuse Charlayne of snubbing the Athens Negro community and, occasionally, the Atlanta Negro community as well. A Charlayne fan might say that Charlayne was really bearing the brunt of the integration, since she lived on campus and maintained contact with white students rather than with Athens Negroes. Most Atlanta Negroes were genuinely proud of both pioneers, but some—so Charlayne and Hamilton were occasionally informed—were tired of hearing about either of them.

Charlayne and Hamilton, who had not been close friends in high school, often seemed to have been driven farther apart by the tensions of Athens and Atlanta. Hamilton sometimes regarded Charlayne as snobbish, irresponsible, and spoiled, and Charlayne sometimes regarded Hamilton as unperceptive, self-satisfied, and ever so slightly square. Weeks passed when they didn't see each other, and now and then they were formally not speaking. Still, like the only two high-school classmates in any big university, they sought each other out in time of trouble or celebration. Charlayne made her most frequent trips to Killian's, where she was uncomfortable, and where Hamilton occasionally accused her of snubbing the boys who played basketball with him, during the bad spring.

As Charlayne and Hamilton began their final quarter, they were agreed on one thing at least—they were glad that the end was in sight. Although Hamilton would be the first Negro in Emory Medical School, he expected no trouble, and he would be living with his family in Atlanta. Charlayne planned to work for a magazine in New York after graduation, and had no desire to return to the South. "This hasn't really been a bad experience," she told me the night before I left Athens. "I've benefited from it, and I think everybody ought to try to be a bit selfish about these things. I'm not bitter. But," she added, "I'm sick of Negroes and sick of white people. I just want to be obscure."

"Everybody here is just delighted to be over the hill," a Georgia professor told me one day at lunch just before I left Georgia, and that summed up the attitude of most of the faculty and administration as Charlayne and Hamilton approached commencement. Everybody seemed happy at having weathered a crisis that could have meant violence and educational chaos. Even those few whose behavior at the time had been disgraceful remarked on how well Georgia had come out of it, especially compared to Mississippi.

Occasionally a university official who was talking about Charlayne and Hamilton would note with some gratitude that neither had been a troublemaker, as if, in the back of his mind, he was as thankful that Georgia had not drawn James H. Meredith as Charlayne and Hamilton were that they had not drawn Ole Miss. The remark was often made with a slight smile, as if of secret understanding—a smile that I had seen on the faces of admissions officials testifying during the trial. Its apparent purpose was to inform the listener that the speaker knew perfectly well that it was all part of the plot—that the

N.A.A.C.P. had conspired to thrust upon the University of Georgia two particularly bright and attractive Negroes, and that, as part of the conspiracy, the two Negroes had reacted to a difficult situation with remarkable poise and maturity. It was just what one might have expected of them. "They have both been very cooperative," William Simpson, the university public-relations man, told me, smiling. "They haven't stirred anything up; they haven't tried to antagonize anybody. It's been to their advantage, of course. They've had good legal advice all the way."

The behavior that evoked expressions of relief from the administration seemed to evoke a detached respect from some of the students. Both responses were complicated by what Carl Holman calls "the anomalous feeling of whites who are against that Negro who has broken the taboo but are drawn by the natural American interest in a celebrity." Holman first became aware of the phenomenon when he and Charlayne were representing the *Inquirer* at a press conference held at the close of the day on which the Atlanta public schools were peacefully desegregated. The police chief of Atlanta informed Holman that he had never talked to Charlayne and would be very much interested in meeting her. I had noticed a less friendly but still genuine interest and curiosity on the part of even the most abusive fraternity members I talked with about Charlayne and Hamilton. The two of them were, after all, the most famous students on the campus, and, in fact, might have been among the most famous people who had ever gone to Georgia—four generations of Talmadges naturally excepted.

One day during my visit, I went to see John Drewry, who has been dean of the Henry W. Grady School of Journalism since 1940. Like most journalism schools, the University of Georgia's school is conscious of its image. It

administers the Peabody Radio and Television awards in
a dignified manner every year, invites important guests to
press institutes, and is proud to give any visitor a list of
its successful alumni. Dean Drewry is a dapper, pen-
guinish man with courtly manners and a soporific Southern drawl. He assured me that Charlayne's stay in the
Journalism School had been "perfectly normal," and that
he had been most happy to see her "make that connection" in New York. He explained that he had attended
Columbia University, in New York, with Chinese, Japa-
nese, and all manner of exotic students (not to speak of
the broadening experience of having attended the Peabody Awards dinners at such places as the Hotel Astor).
The journalism students, he said, had consistently made
the highest scores on the university's intelligence test
ever since 1928, and he suggested that "there may be
some correlation between intelligence and behavior."

"I see her out in the hall talking to other students," the
dean said of Charlayne. "She has attended classes like all
the others, completely free of incident. I believe she'll tell
you that she's been treated just like any other student in
the school. I've been just as kind and considerate, just as
detached and formal. She has conducted herself very
well. I don't think they would have sent anyone but a person of more than average intelligence to be the first. She
has traveled a lot. I believe she had some previous con-
nections, and then the N.A.C.C.—you know what I'm
talking about—arranged some speaking engagements,
I'm sure."

It seemed to me that the dean's courtliness was slip-
ping; white Southerners often have difficulty with the
names of Negro organizations, presumably on the theory
that if they are mispronounced often enough they will go
away.

A moment later, Dean Drewry said, "Here, look—

here's something very interesting." Coming out from behind his desk, he reached into a bookshelf, and then sat
down on a chair beside me, holding a large, elaborately
designed, expensively printed book called *Milestones to
American Liberty: The Foundations of the Republic*. He
read the title aloud, formally, and told me that the book
was a recent one and a very good one. "Look here," he
said, riffling through the pages. "Here's Thomas Paine,
John Peter Zenger, Thomas Jefferson. See, here's some of
Jefferson's writing. And Woodrow Wilson, you remember
him. Here's a picture of Wilson. And look here, on page
two hundred and nine." After a brief glance at the table
of contents, he had turned to a chapter on school desegregation, which included a photograph of Charlayne and
Hamilton. "And here, by golly," the Dean said proudly,
pointing at the picture of Charlayne, "here is a graduate
of the Henry W. Grady School of Journalism."

Epilogue

On June 1, 1963, Charlayne and Hamilton received their degrees from the University cf Georgia and, for a day or two, became Student Heroes again. A picture of them in their academic caps and gowns was widely published, and a television network flew them to New York so they could discuss their experiences at Georgia on an afternoon television show.

Three months later, just after Labor Day week end, Charlayne was back in the news, more famous—or, in her terms, less obscure—than ever. She acknowledged the truth of a rumor that had been circulating in Atlanta throughout the summer—that she and Walter Stovall III, the white journalism student with whom she had often been seen riding around the campus and eating lunch at the Continuing Education Center during her last quarter at Georgia, had been secretly married that spring. Stovall, a soft-spoken twenty-five-year-old Army veteran, was the son of a well-to-do chicken-feed manufacturer and prominent citizen of Douglas, a town of about nine thousand in south Georgia. The marriage had been kept secret until he finished a summer job in Atlanta and joined Charlayne in New York.

Roy Wilkins, the executive secretary of the N.A.A.C.P., told a television reporter, "I expect the opposition, being what it is, to try to ride it high, wide, and handsome. They'll say, 'This proves our point.' But, of course, we don't think it does prove the point. There will be a certain number of intermarriages. Let's face it. But of all the tens of thousands of Negroes that have gone to college in the north, east, and west over all these years, the percentage of intermarriage has been infinitesimal." The loudest reaction in Georgia came, as predicted, from the extreme racists. A restaurant keeper who regularly buys space in the Atlanta *Constitution* to advertise fried chicken and racial purity said, "I Told You So," in precisely those words, and Roy Harris, the university regent who had objected most vigorously to the integration, decried the marriage throughout most of two issues of the Augusta *Courier*, a small paper he publishes to air his views. Although the governor of Georgia commented, when asked, that the marriage was a disgrace, there seemed to be remarkably few public statements from Southern politicians. The attorney general of Georgia, noting that Georgia (like twenty other states) has a law against miscegenation, launched a brief but noisy investigation, and the president of the University of Georgia, O. C. Aderhold, appearing almost as shocked as he had been when Mrs. Motley suggested in court that the university had discriminated against Negro applicants, promised that neither Charlayne nor her husband would be allowed to return to the campus. (Stovall lacked a few credits for his degree, but he had no plans to return. Charlayne, of course, had already been graduated; she was working in New York and was expecting a baby.)

Most of the news stories in the North concentrated on how much damage an interracial marriage involving one of the Student Heroes might do to the Cause, which in these instances is usually spoken of as solely a public-relations campaign rather than an attempt to redress legal wrongs. One or two conservative Washington columnists stated flatly that fear of intermarriage was the principal cause of Southern white resistance to integration and implied that the resistance was now bound to stiffen. Others argued that the Cause would benefit in the long run by the issue of intermarriage being brought out in the open, and that the reality of what was often referred to as "the specter of intermarriage"—a reality that turned out to be one nice-looking, respectable white boy and one nice-looking, respectable Negro girl getting married—must have seemed to Southern whites much less horrible than the visions that had been conjured up by the phrase over the years. Many Negroes and white liberals discussed the marriage more or less as they would have discussed the marriage of the Duke of Windsor; they regretted that it had happened and wondered whether or not Charlayne should have given it up for the Cause. Pointing out the sacrifices that Charlayne had made previously, the Atlanta *Inquirer,* her old paper, asked, "Did Charlayne, because of the key role she accepted from history, have a special obligation or responsibility to make additional personal sacrifices?" The *Inquirer* could find no answer, only a personal decision: "Charlayne simply did not elect additional personal sacrifice."

Charlayne herself was interested to note how few of the people she had told of the marriage during the summer had bothered to wish her happiness before beginning an analysis of how the Cause would be affected. And the day after the marriage was revealed, her answer to the questions of television reporters on the subject reflected the attitude that had been building for two and a half years. "This is a personal thing," Charlayne said, "and my personal life should not have anything to do with that which affects the masses of people. And so I can't be too terribly concerned about that, because I have my own life to live."

There had been other, less publicized developments at the University of Georgia after I returned to New York. For one thing, it turned out that the Reverend William Adams, the minister of the First Presbyterian Church in Athens, had spoken too soon when he told me that Harold Black's integration into First Church might serve as a demonstration to others in the South "that things can be worked out." A few weeks after our conversation, Adams met with Harold Black and, explaining that First Church would continue to seat all visitors, outlined to Harold the possibility of violence and the damage to the church that might be caused by his continued attendance. Harold decided not to return. When I phoned Adams from New York, he told me that pressure had increased since the Sunday Harold sat next to the white girl and the Sunday, a couple of weeks later, when he brought one of the Negro freshman girls with him. Harold had not been forbidden to come, Adams emphasized, and might return in the fall. "I think we did pretty well, considering all things," he said. "We've managed to maintain the official church policy of everybody being welcome. I think we'll do better next time." Some later news from Athens reflected movement in the other direction; in the fall of 1963, the Clarke County school board voluntarily and peacefully began the desegregation of the Athens public schools.

At about the same time that I spoke to Adams, I received a letter from Dean William Tate announcing that Hamilton had been elected to Phi Beta Kappa and sending along a form letter that Tate, as secretary of the Georgia Phi Beta Kappa chapter, had sent to Hamilton. It said, in part, "I am authorized by a ballot of the society to extend to you membership because of your scholastic record here, because your course was interpreted by the Elections Committee as generally liberal in nature, and because your activities and conduct here have been above criticism." Tate had enclosed the letter because it was mentioned in a column by Eugene Patterson, the editor of the Atlanta *Constitution*. Patterson's column, which was also enclosed, began "Dean Bill Tate literally fought Hamilton Holmes' way into the University of Georgia. . . . Now, three years later, the dean had written Holmes a letter informing him that he, the first Negro boy admitted to a white Georgia school, has been elected to Phi Beta Kappa." Patterson continued, "James Meredith has had academic troubles at Ole Miss. Four of the six Negroes at Georgia Tech are struggling to stave off failure. The few Southerners who might be unfeeling enough to try to use this to prove a point for school segregation are simply missing the point of desegregation. This is a land of the lone man, the individual. Americans aren't weighed in bulk. They are measured singly. Their rights include the right to fail. But when desegregation gives one single American the right to succeed, whereas segregation of his whole race would have hobbled him, the point of individual rights, and the worth of the U.S. Constitution, is proved."

On June 6, five days after he had gone to Athens to see his grandson graduate Phi Beta Kappa from the University of Georgia, Dr. Hamilton Mayo Holmes passed a milestone of his own. It occurred on the Macon public golf course, which had been peacefully desegregated two years before, without even the help of a lawsuit or a member of the Holmes family. Playing in a foursome that included Oliver Wendell Holmes, who told me the story, Dr. Holmes, by that time seventy-nine years old, finished the course with a score of exactly seventy-nine—and finally, after twenty-nine years of trying, shot his age.